FEBRUARY 2017

Science, Technology, and U.S. National Security Strategy

Preparing Military Leadership for the Future

PRINCIPAL AUTHOR
Raymond F. DuBois

CONTRIBUTING AUTHORS
Daniel M. Gerstein
James M. Keagle

FOREWORD
Admiral James Stavridis (USN Ret.)

AFTERWORD
John J. Hamre

RESEARCH ASSISTANT
Rose Morrissy

CSIS | CENTER FOR STRATEGIC & INTERNATIONAL STUDIES

ROWMAN & LITTLEFIELD
Lanham • Boulder • New York • London

About CSIS

For over 50 years, the Center for Strategic and International Studies (CSIS) has worked to develop solutions to the world's greatest policy challenges. Today, CSIS scholars are providing strategic insights and bipartisan policy solutions to help decisionmakers chart a course toward a better world.

CSIS is a nonprofit organization headquartered in Washington, D.C. The Center's 220 full-time staff and large network of affiliated scholars conduct research and analysis and develop policy initiatives that look into the future and anticipate change.

Founded at the height of the Cold War by David M. Abshire and Admiral Arleigh Burke, CSIS was dedicated to finding ways to sustain American prominence and prosperity as a force for good in the world. Since 1962, CSIS has become one of the world's preeminent international institutions focused on defense and security; regional stability; and transnational challenges ranging from energy and climate to global health and economic integration.

Thomas J. Pritzker was named chairman of the CSIS Board of Trustees in November 2015. Former U.S. deputy secretary of defense John J. Hamre has served as the Center's president and chief executive officer since 2000.

CSIS does not take specific policy positions; accordingly, all views expressed herein should be understood to be solely those of the author(s).

© 2017 by the Center for Strategic and International Studies. All rights reserved.

ISBN: 978-1-4422-8007-6 (pb); 978-1-4422-8008-3 (eBook)

Center for Strategic & International Studies
1616 Rhode Island Avenue, NW
Washington, DC 20036
202-887-0200 | www.csis.org

Rowman & Littlefield
4501 Forbes Boulevard
Lanham, MD 20706
301-459-3366 | www.rowman.com

Contents

IV   Foreword, *Admiral James Stavridis (USN Ret.)*

V   Acknowledgments

VI   Executive Summary

1   Science, Technology, and U.S. National Security Strategy: Preparing Military Leadership for the Future

1   Introduction

1   Background and Study Genesis

2   The Importance of Science and Technology

4   The Case for Change

4   Curriculum for Science and Technology in Military Education Programs

5   Why Professional Military Education and Human Resources/Talent Management?

7   The Joint Professional Military Education Conundrum

7   A Way Forward

9   Afterword, *Dr. John J. Hamre*

10   Appendix A. Curriculum for Science and Technology in Military Education Programs

13   Appendix B. Curricula Offered at the War Colleges That Relate to S&T and Strategy

16   Appendix C. First CSIS Roundtable Participants (July 25, 2016)

17   Appendix D. Second CSIS Roundtable Participants (October 17, 2016)

18   Appendix E. Individuals Who Provided Input, But Did Not Participate in CSIS Roundtables

23   Bibliography

42   About the Authors

Foreword

While I have spent most of my intellectual life in the social sciences—studying international relations and earning a PhD in international law—it is quite clear to me that science and technology are an enormous part of our ability to protect the United States. We need the teaching of Thucydides, Clausewitz, and Mahan—but also the lessons of Edison, Einstein, and Faraday.

The key is finding the right balance between the study of strategy, policy, tactics, history, and other traditional military disciplines and the hard sciences, especially in emerging fields like artificial intelligence, computational science, biosynthetics, genomics, robotics, nanotechnology, and advanced materials.

To create security in this turbulent twenty-first century, we will require officers skilled in science and technology who are initially tracked into these fields, continue to learn throughout their careers, and are given ample opportunity to interact with the private sector, where so many of the most important advances occur.

In this superb and concise study of how best to create that cadre of officers, the authors lay out a practical, systemic, and logical path. We should follow it carefully, and invest intelligently with the very best of our human capital.

Admiral James Stavridis (USN Ret.)
Dean, The Fletcher School of Law and Diplomacy
Tufts University

Acknowledgments

The Center for Strategic and International Studies (CSIS) would like to thank the Richard Lounsbery Foundation for its generous support of this study, as well as the MD5 National Security Technology Accelerator for its support of this second-phase study. The first-phase study published by CSIS in November 2015, *Science, Technology, and U.S. National Security Strategy: The Role of the War Colleges*, was also funded by the Richard Lounsbery Foundation.

Raymond F. DuBois, resident senior adviser at CSIS, managed this project and coauthored the final report with Dr. Daniel M. Gerstein and Dr. James M. Keagle. The authors wish to thank the CSIS publications staff and in particular to thank Admiral James Stavridis (USN Ret.) and Dr. John Hamre for their contributions to the report.

The authors would also like to thank the participants of the two roundtables held at CSIS (see Appendices C and D). Finally, the authors would like to thank the many former and current government officials and academic experts who provided input to the report (see Appendix E).

Executive Summary

The United States has long sought qualitative military superiority to deter the next war, and if necessary, to fight and win that contest. Developing, acquiring, and then sustaining technological advantages over our adversaries has been part of that strategy since World War II, along with our heavy reliance on the quantitative muscle that the arsenal of democracy provided.

Today's imperative is to identify, adapt, and field advanced technologies with military applications. This initiative is often referred to as the "Third Offset." Unlike the first two offset strategies that provided enduring, albeit now less competitive edges, this Third Offset will be driven by much faster-paced technological changes. In Gen. Joe Dunford's words, "There is no substitute for leadership that recognizes the implications of new ideas, new technologies and new approaches and actually anticipates the effects of those adaptations."[1] It also demands a culture of experimentation that embraces failure where it is thoughtful and considered since the path ahead is not known. In our judgment, it also must include complementary professional military education (PME) and human resources/talent management (HR) systems and processes to promote creative and critical strategic thinkers.

A dominant theme of the twenty-first century is the democratization of science and technology (S&T). It is a driving force throughout global society and pervasive throughout all aspects of human endeavor, to include national security. High-technology weapons are no longer the exclusive domain of only a few nations. Smaller states are expanding their arsenals and infusing advanced technologies into their warfighting tactics, operations, and strategy. The democratization of technology has also given some nonstate actors (from small groups to individuals) access to capabilities that in the past have only been reserved for nation states. Indeed, the technologies of destruction and the attendant increased capabilities of communication and surveillance, create a threat landscape unlike any we have faced.

In this challenging, technologically informed environment, the U.S. military must continue to ensure a competitive advantage. One of the ways to do so is to develop a cadre of technologically competent officers with the requisite leadership and operational skills to excel in this fast-paced and ever-evolving environment. It involves a complementary set of selection, assignment, promotion, and military and civilian education opportunities that infuse our next generation of leaders with strategic, creative, and critical thinking attributes to interact effectively between and among the policy, technology, and operational communities.

In short, what is needed is a system that allows a group of these select officers to move between operational and S&T tracks throughout their careers. The end goal is the creation of a cohort that has demonstrated excellence in both fields, and that is able to reach the highest levels of the military and national security communities. It also strongly suggests that the entire

---

[1] Jim Garamone, "Dunford to NDU Grads: Embrace Change and Innovation," *DoD News*, June 9, 2016, http://www.defense.gov/News/Article/Article/795572/dunford-to-ndu-grads-embrace-change-and-innovation.

force be more sensitized to the S&T world, so that as a minimum, they will recognize the tactical, operational, and strategic applications of emerging sciences and technologies, and understand the value they offer against legacy systems, operational concepts, and doctrines. This goal needs to be accomplished without building additional career tracks and yet not subsuming S&T under the acquisition career field where it is likely to lose some sharpness of focus and connectedness to national security strategy and be restricted to those branch-selected officers.

Preparing our leadership for the challenges and opportunities of S&T carries with it a central role for education—who gets what, how much, and when.

Specifically, joint professional military education (JPME) is faced with internal challenges to its own relevancy in its task of delivering the right material, with appropriate methodologies, at the right times, to the right people. While bedrock seminal content such as Thucydides, Clausewitz, Mahan, or Boyd will endure as critical elements of the curricula over generations, other academic content is more transient as the security environment evolves. Equally important, academic methodologies must adopt techniques that best leverage the learning styles of the upcoming leadership generation (and by implication apply cognitive science to JPME).

In our judgment, one of the Chairman of the Joint Chiefs of Staff's Desired Leader Attributes (DLA)[2] should be the ability to "understand the scientific method and apply it to the challenges of innovation and emerging technologies."

A Way Forward

Among the steps to be considered:

1. Design early opportunities with identifiable secondary career tracks and promotional opportunities for individuals to self or be system-selected to specialize in S&T; these career tracks must have reasonable promotion potential.
2. Craft academic programs that build on each other throughout one's career, culminating with strategic level perspectives and abilities to integrate S&T knowledge across disciplines and with policy.
3. Create improved opportunities for officers to interact and cross-pollinate with the industrial sector and the extensive government laboratory system—both their ideas and their people.
4. Utilize tier-one private and public universities for specific advanced degree S&T offerings and programs in lieu of, or in partnership with, existing PME schools. This should also include leveraging Service ROTC programs to introduce specific S&T topics into curricula and providing more content direction for those pursuing graduate education.
5. Allow selected officers greater freedom of movement between operational and S&T assignments and educational opportunities to build a cadre of officers able to perform at the highest military levels and have private-sector networks and relationships.

---

[2] See list of current DLAs in "Chairman of the Joint Chiefs of Staff Instruction 1800.01E: Officer Professional Military Education Policy," May 29, 2015, A2–A3, http://www.dtic.mil/doctrine/education/officer_JPME/cjcsi1800_01e.pdf.

Science and Technology: The pace of scientific and technological (S&T) innovation over the past 100 years has been astounding. Rapid advances in medical, biological, computing, cognition, physics, chemistry, materiel science, aerospace, energy, and many other fields have benefited the world—and also benefited the Joint Force and U.S. Army. As our Army seeks to preserve or extend its dominance into the twenty-first century, how should we think about the role of science and technology? Will the rate of S&T innovation continue to accelerate into the future and provide us opportunities to exploit—or is the rate of S&T innovation slowing down? Are new or different S&T fields more promising than others from a military standpoint?[3]

Mark A. Milley
General, U.S. Army Chief of Staff

---

[3] U.S. Army War College, *Key Strategic Issues List: Academic Year 2016–2017* (Carlisle, PA: U.S. Army War College Press, July 2016), 9, http://www.strategicstudiesinstitute.army.mil/pdffiles/PUB1334.pdf.

Science, Technology, and U.S. National Security Strategy

Preparing Military Leadership for the Future

Introduction

The United States has long sought qualitative military superiority to deter the next war, and if necessary, to fight and win that contest. Simply put, the United States does not want a fair fight among equal forces, but rather it seeks to end wars quickly and decisively. Obtaining and then sustaining technological advantages over our adversaries has been part of that strategy since World War II, along with our heavy reliance on the quantitative muscle that the arsenal of democracy provided.

The First Offset and Second Offset are two distinct periods in our post–World War II national security posture that exemplify our evolving qualitative superiority strategy:

- The First Offset relied on the threatened use of battlefield nuclear weapons to counter the quantitative advantages of the Soviet Union's and Warsaw Pact's conventional forces;

- The subsequent Second Offset relied on the application of global positioning systems (GPS) to precision-guided munitions and stealthy delivery platforms to again address quantitative shortfalls against potential adversaries.

Today's emphasis is to find that next, Third Offset. Emanating from Secretary of Defense Chuck Hagel's 2014 defense innovation initiative, Secretary of Defense Ash Carter and Deputy Secretary of Defense Bob Work describe the Third Offset as part innovation, part investment in science and technology (S&T), and part entrepreneurial spirit to find those disruptive, game-changing and force-multiplying capabilities, and then to craft their associated operating concepts. Unlike the first two offset strategies that provided enduring but diminishing competitive edges, this Third Offset will be driven by much faster-paced technological change. In Secretary Carter's words, "The race now depends on who can out-innovate faster than anyone else." It also demands a culture of experimentation that embraces failure where it was thoughtful and considered since the path ahead is not known (Elon Musk to Secretary Carter, June 2016). In our judgment, it also must include complementary professional military education (PME) and human resources (HR) systems and processes to promote creative and critical strategic thinkers.

Background and Study Genesis

CSIS originally proposed a study that looked at addressing both an understanding of emerging S&T possibilities and a grasp of S&T investment strategies and S&T expertise within the U.S.

defense enterprise. After completing the first study, it was decided a follow-up study that offered a more detailed set of options to incorporate science and technology more deeply into the national security strategy thinking of our nation's future military and civilian leaders would be beneficial.

The Importance of Science and Technology

America's global strategic leadership rests on a strong foundation of science and technology, which has contributed to our political, economic, and military dominance throughout much of the twentieth and into the twenty-first centuries. Perfecting industrial age capacities, including techniques for mass production, contributed to both our economic development and our victory in World War II. In addition, our ability to develop and relatively quickly field state-of-the-art military capabilities—culminating with the development of the atomic bomb—contributed immeasurably to the Allied victory. After 1945 our ability to project power across the globe was unmatched. The United States was the leader in global affairs as well as in science and technology.

In this World War II era, research and development was connected to operational requirements. In the postwar years, deliberate decisions were made to have dedicated locations for basic research to flourish. The National Science Foundation was an outgrowth of this thinking. The precursors to the Department of Energy labs were critical to the Manhattan Project, and the Department of Defense Service labs were seen as an important investment in more focused research and development, aligned to the missions of their parent organizations. Yet a constant tension ensued between these labs that sought to conduct science for the sake of discovery and the desire to have operational outcomes as by-products of these significant investments. The Defense Advanced Research Projects Agency (DARPA) formed in 1958—in the aftermath of the Soviet's Sputnik rocket launch—was an attempt to get back to a connected model where science and technology was tied to operational requirements.

Today the United States confronts a different world in which science and technology is globalized. The barriers for conducting research and development have been reduced. The competitive advantage the United States enjoyed in the post–World War II era has been eroded as more nations are investing in research and development. U.S. government and overall U.S. share of R&D is shrinking as a percent of global R&D. Neither large multinational corporations nor small start-ups can claim to be the exclusive leaders in research and development. However, each has an important role to play in the development and fielding of technological advances.

Equally important, the industrial age that defined the period of the Cold War has been replaced by an information age where flows of information and ideas occur in milliseconds. Assured communications allow for instantaneous direction of the elements of national power. Advanced technology allows for owning the night through use of advanced optics and night vision devices, fielding ubiquitous networks that fuse vast amounts of data for warfighting commanders across the globe, and employing precision effects for achieving U.S. goals and objectives. However, the United States is no longer the only nation with these capabilities and in some cases is no longer the dominant nation in some fields.

The changes occurring around the globe mandate a different way of thinking about technology and maintaining our competitive advantage. The Department of Defense can no longer think of conducting its research and development internally in all areas of interest. Rather in select areas, the DoD must rely on industry for R&D. Examples include biotechnology, cyber and information technology, and even the space industry. In other areas led by the DoD, investments will be required to provide the necessary capabilities. The trick will be to differentiate between these different types of technology areas.

Efforts such as Joint Vision 2010 mandated by Chairman of the Joint Chiefs of Staff, General John Shalikashvili, that led to the development of the Joint Requirements Oversight Council (JROC), the Department of Defense various transformation efforts undertaken at the Service levels in 1999–2002 and more recently the Defense Digital Service (DDS) and the Defense Innovation Unit Experimental (DIUx) are efforts to align research, development, and acquisition with operational or warfighting requirements.

A related topic receiving important emphasis by senior DoD leaders and within the operational force is innovation. Innovation is inextricably linked to science and technology, and in many instances the terms are used interchangeably. Yet there are also nuanced differences that are worthy of highlighting.

The reason for the confusion largely relates to the perceived similarities between technology and innovation. Technology is the application of scientific knowledge for practical purposes, while innovation is the process of translating ideas or inventions into something of value. Both seek to provide practical solutions to problems. So the distinction between technology development and innovation comes down to whether the application stems from scientific knowledge (as in the case of technology development) or from an idea or invention (as in the case of innovation). However, both are engineering disciplines that use applied principles in search of solutions to operational problems.

Both S&T and innovation are nonlinear processes. That is, discovery and creativity do not proceed in a linear manner, but rather have a recursive nature. As discoveries are made or innovations adopted, invariably they lead to other innovations.

An important distinction between S&T and innovation surrounds how these efforts proceed within organizations. S&T derives from a formal process, where important areas of interest receive support for investigation and discovery. Links to operational problems are important, but not always a driving force, such as in the case of basic research that seeks to gain an understanding of a phenomenon without regard to a specific application or outcome.

In contrast, innovation directly relates to satisfying operational needs. It depends on having a deep understanding of operations and looking for better ways to accomplish a task or new approaches to improving operational effectiveness and efficiency. Innovation is also about the free flow of ideas and the culture of the organization. For organizations to embrace innovation means that trial and error must be allowed, even embraced. "Failures" provide opportunities for reevaluation, reflection, and perhaps even return to first principles. This is not to say that innovation lacks discipline, but rather that by nature it is freer flowing than S&T. Secretary Carter's establishment of the Strategic Capabilities Office (SCO) will drive this innovation culture.

This effort focuses directly on S&T and by inference on innovation. It makes the case that the ability to understand the scientific method and apply it to operational challenges is a critical skill for the joint officer, now and in the future. It also makes the case that additional skills will be required for applying the S&T lens to analyzing operational concepts with longer-range policies, strategies, and resource decisions. And most importantly, it highlights the necessity of developing a culture of experimentation, risk taking, and failure (fail early and often).

So the ultimate question is: In such a world where science and technology features so prominently, how can the military develop the capacity for recruiting, training and educating, developing, nurturing, and ultimately retaining leaders with the intellectual depth and curiosity and operational acumen to lead today and into the future.

The Case for Change

A dominant theme of the twenty-first century is the democratization of science and technology. It is a driving force throughout global society and pervasive throughout all aspects of human endeavor, to include national security. High-technology weapons are no longer the exclusive domain of only a few nations. Smaller countries are expanding their arsenals and infusing advanced technologies into their warfighting tactics, operations, and strategy. The democratization of technology has also given some nonstate actors (from small groups to individuals) access to capabilities that in the past have only been reserved for nation-states.

In this challenging, technologically informed environment, the U.S. military must continue to ensure a competitive advantage. One of the ways to do so is to develop a cadre of technologically competent officers with the requisite leadership and operational skills to excel in this fast-paced and ever-evolving environment.

In sum, what is needed is a personnel system that allows a group of these select officers to move between the operational and S&T tracks throughout their careers. The end goal is the creation of a cohort that has demonstrated excellence in both fields, and is able to reach the highest levels of the military. It also strongly suggests that the entire force be more sensitized to the S&T world, so that as a minimum, they will recognize the tactical, operational, and strategic applications of emerging sciences and technologies, and understand the value they offer against legacy systems, operational concepts, and doctrines. This needs to be accomplished without building additional career tracks and yet not subsuming S&T under the acquisition career fields where it is likely to lose some sharpness of focus and connectedness to national security strategy and be restricted to those branch-selected officers.

Curricula for Science and Technology in Military Education Programs

Given the emerging importance of S&T to national security decisions, both policy and acquisition, inclusion in the JPME curricula becomes a natural extension. In thinking about what level of engagement in the subject is necessary and desirable from an organizational and personnel perspective, one can conclude that a single approach would be highly limiting. While all students would benefit from a working knowledge of the importance of S&T, others would likely desire to have a greater exposure to and understanding of the topic.

Therefore, in developing a program, several principles should apply. First, all students should have an introduction into the topics of S&T in national security affairs. Second, students might desire to self-select into a deeper examination of the topic. Still others might have a desire to participate in a concentration in the S&T field. Third, regardless of which track a student might decide to pursue, emphasis can be made by infusing S&T discussions into current topics with minimal overhead; an example would be to have an S&T-related learning objective in current courses being offered. Finally, the teaching methodology should be in keeping with the focus on seminars, augmented with lectures as required. The curricula will entail a mix of active and passive learning, but will be designed to maximize student engagement in the learning process. Representative curricula overviews for the three levels of participation are provided in Appendix A. They are meant to be illustrative and not prescriptive.

The curricula target the senior service college level. However, exposure to S&T should begin much earlier in an officer's career. Ultimately, this would be more in keeping with the goals of developing a technologically informed joint force able both to understand and operate in a dangerously competitive world. The democratization of technology has narrowed the United States' comparative advantages in technology and even allowed potentially dangerous technologies to proliferate, leading in some cases to nonstate actors having state-like capabilities.

Why Professional Military Education and Human Resources/Talent Management?

The military officer of today faces a complex and dynamic environment that requires an increasingly broader set of intellectual capacities and experiences. Training in one's basic military skill area remains necessary, but is not sufficient for the individual, his or her service, or the Department of Defense.

Becoming an expert in a warfighting domain requires training, education, and experiences in a defined area. Examples, such as aviation, have significant upfront investment, require maintaining and improving skills over the length of a career, and the development of tacit knowledge that allows for leadership and command at higher levels. The same can be said for submarine and surface warfare officers in the Navy or infantry and armor officers in the Army and Marines. This specialization requires time and management to ensure that the proper individual and leadership development occurs.

Yet at the 0-4/5 level, a transition should occur where the ability to think more broadly and abstractly takes on an increased importance. During this period of an officer's career, demands begin to move away from the more-focused skill sets developed in initial operational training, education, and experiences, and instead moves toward complex skills across a more strategic landscape. For example, the pilot assigned to the joint staff as a planner might be required to participate in an arms-control negotiation on nuclear, chemical, or biological weapons. Or perhaps this individual will be required to have an understanding of the complexities of cybersecurity for a military plan being developed.

However, today's career-management system values specialization over broader experiences and requires officers to select or be selected for repetitive assignments in their basic branches or specialties. In some cases, officers deviating from this specialization model are discouraged or even penalized for developing, albeit important, "secondary skills." This system in many cases—either by career timelines or by assignment requirements—can even prohibit movement between operational and nonoperational career paths. True dual-track opportunities are indeed challenging both to create and for the select officers (and NCOs) to pursue and maintain. But they are necessary. Moreover, some intervention, likely at the service secretary level, is necessary to ensure that promotion boards receive instructions designed to reward—and promote these dual-track specialists—at rates comparable to their peers. This needs to occur well before general officer/flag officer selection boards—perhaps as early as promotion to major/lieutenant commander.

Similarly, in our discussions with senior UK military officers (see Appendix E), it became clear that the emphasis on broader and deeper education opportunities and a focused personnel management system is necessary, In a recent UK Ministry of Defence document it states: "A strategic leader…will be aware of the impact of technology in the delivery of Defence output and have been a practitioner in the career field for which he or she will be responsible." In addition, it continues, "a Service-owned and Service-led robust and objective talent management process is needed…balancing the tension between valuing high performance and developing high potential."[1]

These examples above demonstrate the value of having broader intellectual capacity (the PME mission) and suggest the necessity of expanding beyond the traditional warfighting proficiencies to include a wider variety of skills and thinking. It also points to the challenge of an individual's "career ownership" by specialty career HR managers and specialized mentors within that career field. We must produce the best-educated officer possible with both specialized and generalized intellectual skills. This demands a cradle-to-grave approach—conscientious career management of our officers to ensure the nation can discover and apply the knowledge of today and tomorrow to the art and science of war and statecraft.

Waiting until the War College experience is simply too late. This needs to be a priority in our pre-commissioning programs, even reaching into our high schools and JROTC-like programs. Also, we need to leverage and expand existing programs that identify selected officers for special tracking, assignments, education, and other professional development and utilization tours. While restricted to just a few officers, the assignment to gain a master's or doctoral degree in order to teach at a service academy is such a program.

---

[1] "Defense Education Pathway Review: Summary v5 1230," April 8, 2016, 5. Unpublished draft shared with author.

The Joint Professional Military Education Conundrum

Preparing our leadership for the challenges and opportunities of S&T carries with it a central role for education—who gets what, how much, and when.

Specifically, joint professional military education (JPME) is faced with internal challenges to its own relevancy in its task of delivering the right material, with appropriate methodologies, at the right times, to the right people. While bedrock seminal content such as Thucydides, Clausewitz, Mahan, or Boyd will endure as critical elements of the curricula over generations, other academic content is more transient as the security environment evolves. Equally important, academic methodologies must also adjust to today's different learning styles. Moreover, increasingly complex problems require multidisciplinary skills and agile minds—truly Renaissance thinkers.

While JPME may be able to address these academic problems, personnel-management systems and service cultures/subcultures constrain opportunities for success. Promotion and assignment rules, regulations, and cultural traditions affect what can be offered, and the student's perceptions of what should be taken. Paths that would broaden perspectives and peripheral interests are often rejected in favor of those that reinforce and deepen more myopic points of view unique to the individual's early-on identified career field (specialty). Said another way, the military typecasts too early, does not reward broadening experiences, and in fact promotes those who principally if not exclusively develop and then remain loyal (trapped) to their narrow, essentially stove-piped, specializations. Opportunities for rounding are limited—and perceived as disloyal acts, particularly given the costs associated with producing specialists.

To overcome such obstacles, earlier and more frequent opportunities for well-roundedness need to be balanced against the legitimate need to develop and maintain credibility and deep subject-matter operational expertise. Absent that, the war colleges will inherit and produce a student population year after year that is ill-prepared to effectively bridge both the tactical and operational with the strategic, and to bridge technologies with policy.

JPME does have a central role in this process along with complementary HR department processes.

A Way Forward

Among the steps to be considered:

1. Design early opportunities with identifiable career tracks and promotional opportunities for individuals to self or be system-selected to specialize in S&T; these must have reasonable promotion potential;

2. Craft academic programs that build on each other throughout one's career, culminating with strategic-level perspectives and abilities to integrate S&T knowledge across disciplines and with policy.

3. Create improved opportunities for officers to interact and cross-pollinate with the private sector—both their ideas and their people. Example: some revival of the secretary of defense corporate fellows program. This program could interact with the secretary of defense's future force concepts of more flexible entry and exit points for military service as well as the natural links to the private sector that the reserve and guard components afford.

4. Utilize tier-one private and public universities for specific S&T advanced degree offerings and programs in lieu of, or in partnership with, existing PME schools. This should include leveraging service ROTC programs to introduce specific S&T topics into curricula and providing more content direction for those pursuing graduate education. It is simply not resource efficient for the military to educate its officer exclusively within its own fences. Furthermore, educational opportunities at civilian universities build additional bridges between the military and civil society.

5. Allow selected officers greater freedom of movement between operational and S&T assignments and educational opportunities to build a cadre of officers who are able to perform at the highest military levels and have private-sector networks and relationships.

Afterword

In the foreword to the phase I study, *Science, Technology, and U.S. National Security Strategy: The Role of the War Colleges* (CSIS, November 2015), I stated that America is now in the most chaotic global environment since the end of the Cold War. America must craft a new grand strategy to meet and overcome the wide range of threats it faces, from cyber defense to counterinsurgency to traditional nation-state security threats to the global order.

This range of threats calls for a far more innovative and dynamic Department of Defense. We have an imperative to identify, adapt, and field advanced technologies at a far faster pace than is our historic norm. In recent years, the Defense Department and the Congress have been creating organizations to help promote innovation—the Defense Innovation Advisory Board, the Strategic Capabilities Office, the Defense Innovation Unit-experimental offices. Congress last year directed the disassembly of the Office of the Under Secretary for Acquisition, Technology and Logistics, in part to heighten the priority of innovation for the department. This year the department will determine how to organize and integrate the stipulated offices created by the National Defense Authorization Act of 2017.

This study looks at leadership—and the role that competent officers and civilians will play to introducing and integrating emerging technologies and advanced sciences into our national security thinking. Organizations are important, but leadership is essential.

It was the late David Abshire who originally proposed this study, and it was he who understood that the human element will always be the key to innovation, determining how best to use and respond to technological advantages in the battlespace, irrespective of domain.

Technology is fundamental to modern warfare. The grand strategy for the Cold War was built on the technological superiority that America used to offset the numerical advantages of the Soviet Union. Now technology is needed to permit the Defense Department to manage a far more complicated and divergent security landscape. This report offers insights into how joint professional military education and human resource systems can promote creative and strategic thinkers who can institutionalize innovation in the department.

John J. Hamre
President and CEO
Center for Strategic and International Studies

Appendix A. Curriculum for Science and Technology in Military Education Programs

Given the emerging importance of S&T to national security leaders, inclusion in the military curriculum becomes a natural extension. In thinking about what level of engagement in the subject is necessary and desirable from an organizational and personnel perspective, one can conclude that a single approach would be highly limiting. While all students would benefit from a working knowledge of the importance of S&T, others would likely desire to have a greater exposure to and understanding of the topic.

Therefore, in developing a program, several principles should apply. First, all students should have an introduction into the topics of S&T in national security affairs. Second, students might desire to self-select into a deeper examination of the topic. Still others might have a desire to participate in a concentration in the S&T field. Third, regardless of which track a student might decide to pursue, emphasis can be made by infusing S&T discussions into current topics with minimal overhead; an example would be to have an S&T-related learning objective in current courses being offered. Finally, the teaching methodology should be in keeping with the focus on seminars, augmented with lectures given by leading innovators and technologists from the public and private sectors. The curriculum will entail a mix of active and passive learning, but will be designed to maximize student engagement in the learning process.

The curricula developed below are targeting the senior service college level. However, exposure to S&T should begin much earlier in an officer's career. Ultimately, this would be more in keeping with the goals of developing a technologically informed joint force able to both understand and operate in a world where the democratization of technology has narrowed the United States' comparative advantages in technology and even allowed potentially dangerous technologies to proliferate leading, in some cases, to nonstate actors having state-like capabilities.

Representative curricula overviews for the three levels of participation are illustrated below. These are meant to be illustrative and not prescriptive:

Module: Introduction to Science & Technology in National Security Affairs

Description: Module would provide a focused discussion on S&T including introduction, definitions, and applications in national security affairs. It would be designed to ensure that students have a working understanding of the topic and support making all students more aware of the national security implications of S&T.

Audience: Entire student body would receive this block of instruction.

How to implement: The CJCS emphasis on a strategic leader foundations course offered in the beginning of the first term at National Defense University senior-level colleges is a logical place to begin to seed S&T. It could be followed by concentration programs, increased S&T focus within relevant industry study programs at the Eisenhower School, and selected electives.

Time: Five hours of seminar and lecture time. Notional topics for the five hours are listed below in the diagram. Incorporating S&T discussions into other courses would increase emphasis on the topic and reinforce the learning objectives of this module as well as to highlight the importance of understanding S&T for national security practitioners. Speakers should include prominent CEOs of leading-edge Fortune 500 firms.

Introduction to Science & Technology	Historical Perspective to S&T in National Security	The Democratization of S&T and What It Means for National Security	Strategies for Managing Technology	Case Studies

Course: Science & Technology in National Security Affairs

Description: Course would include an introduction, definitions, and applications in national security affairs of S&T. The elective would be subdivided into four modules: (1) introduction to S&T, (2) managing S&T, (3) case studies, and (4) future of S&T. The culmination of the course would be a three-hour exercise designed to reinforce the course learning objectives.

Audience: Students self-select into the course.

Time: Forty hours of seminars and lectures.

Introduction to S&T	Managing S&T	Case Studies	Future of S&T
• Introduction • Definitions • Historical Perspective	• Democratization of S&T • Dual-Use • Export Controls • Arms Control	• Case Studies of Various Technologies (e.g., unmanned aerial systems, nuclear fuel cycle)	• Examine Emerging Future S&T • Implications for National Security

Concentration: Science & Technology in National Security Affairs

Description: Concentration would provide a focused opportunity for students to delve into the field of S&T. It would build on the earlier course, science and technology in national security affairs, and be designed to allow students to examine an S&T topic of interest in greater detail.

Audience: Students self-select into the course.

Time: Four electives beginning with the elective discussed above allow students to delve deeply into the S&T field. The other three electives would take the students farther into understanding the implications of S&T on national security issues. Elective #2 would expose students to technologies, beginning with historical perspectives of S&T in national security affairs and concluding with examining emerging technologies. Elective #3 would provide the students with an understanding of how the democratization of technology has fundamentally altered relations between nations and even allowed nonstate actors to have unprecedented capabilities and reach. Finally, Elective #4 would allow the students to select an S&T issue of interest and delve deeply into the technology as is exists today and also into the future.

Elective #1: Science & Technology in National Security Affairs (As Described Above)	Elective #2: Case Studies in S&T • Historical Perspective • Current Trends • Future Issues *3 cases each*	Elective #3: Democratization of S&T • Asymmetric Warfare • Non-State Actors • Third Offset & Innovation	Elective #4: Students select a technology to examine, prepare a paper and provide a presentation to class

Readings would be designed to give students foundations on which to base class discussions. They would expose the students to current principles for understanding the role of technology in a range of societal phenomena and their effect on national security. These readings are representative and not meant to be prescriptive.

- Arthur, Brian W. *The Nature of Technology: What It Is and How It Evolves*. New York: Free Press, 2011.

- Black, Jeremy. *War and Technology*. Bloomington, Indiana: Indiana University Press, 2013.

- Christensen, Clayton M. *The Innovator's Dilemma: The Revolutionary Book That Will Change the Way You Do Business*. New York: HarperBusiness: Reprint edition, 2011.

- McNeill, William H. *The Pursuit of Power: Technology, Armed Force, and Society since A.D. 1000*. Chicago: University of Chicago Press, 1982.

- Parker, Barry. *The Physics of War: From Arrows to Atoms*. Amherst, New York: Prometheus Books, 2014.

- Stokes, Donald E. *Pasteur's Quadrant: Basic Science and Technological Innovation*. Washington, DC: Brookings Institution Press, 1997.

- Selected articles on S&T.

Appendix B. Curricula Offered at the War Colleges That Relate to S&T and Strategy[1]

U.S. Army War College

Center for Strategic Leadership (CSL):

    Cyber Warfare

    Cyber Warfare Planning

    Futures Seminar

    Wargaming for Strategic Leaders

Department of Command, Leadership, and Management (DCLM):

    Creative Leadership

    Strategic Thinking and Leadership

    Leading Innovation

    The Defense Industrial Base

Department of National Security and Strategy (DNSS):

    Crafting a U.S. Grand Strategy for the 21st Century

Department of Military Strategy, Planning, and Operations (DMSPO)

    Cyber Concepts for Senior Leaders (unclassified)

    Cyberspace and Cyber Operations—What Senior Leaders Need to Know

U.S. National War College

Strategic Leadership Foundational Course

Strategic Leadership Foundational Course II

U.S. Naval War College

MAWS[2] I – Naval Warfare and Operational Art

MAWS II – The Navy Planning Process and the JFMCC[3] Environment

MAWS III – Major Operations and Campaigns – Historical Case Studies

War Gaming Theory and Practice

A Critical Analysis of Air Power since WWI

---

[1] This list is not exhaustive.
[2] Maritime Advanced Warfighting School (MAWS).
[3] Joint Force Maritime Component Commander (JFMCC).

Science, Technology and Strategy

Unmanned Systems and Conflict in the 21st Century

Seminar on Space Technology and Policy

Cyber-security: Cybered Conflict, Response to Surprise, and Emerging Indicators of Global System Change

Information Operations and Cyberwarfare

Operations in Cyberspace

Biological and Chemical Agents and Their Use in Warfare and Terrorism

Ethics of Technology: Warfare and Society

Halsey A

Halsey B

Halsey Gravely

Strategy and Policy

U.S. Air War College

Foundations of Strategy

Space Operations

Non-Lethal Weapons: Support to 21st Century Warfare and Homeland Defense

Group Research: Blue Horizons

Group Research: Cyberspace

Grand Strategy Program

    Military Innovation

U.S. Marine Corps War College

National Security and Joint Warfare

Advanced Studies Program

    Future Wars

Dwight D. Eisenhower School for National Security and Resource Strategy

Strategic Leadership Foundational Course

Strategic Leadership Foundational Course II

Defense Strategy, Acquisition, and Resourcing (DSAR) Department

    Strategic Acquisition and Resourcing

National Security and the Industrial Base (NSIB) Department

    Industry Study

Long-Term Strategy Concentration

Adaptive and Agile Leaders Network (AALN) Concentration

Joint and Combined Warfighting School

Preparing for Strategic Surprise: USSTRATCOM[4] perspectives

USSOCOM[5] Joint Special Operations in the 21st Century

Challenges in Cyberspace

College of International Security Affairs

Strategic Thought

U.S. Army Command and General Staff College

Advanced Studies Program

    Contemporary Operational Art

Advanced Strategic Leadership Studies Program

    Twenty-first Century Conflict

---

[4] U.S. Strategic Command (USSTRATCOM).
[5] U.S. Special Forces Command (USSOCOM).

Appendix C. First CSIS Roundtable Participants (July 25, 2016)

Dr. Shannon Brown, *Professor, Industrial College of the Armed Forces, The Eisenhower School, National Defense University*

Col. Susan Bryant, *Army Senior Fellow, Institute for National Strategic Studies, National Defense University*

Dr. R. E. Burnett, *Associate Dean of Academics (Faculty) and Professor, National Defense University*

Ben FitzGerald, *Senior Fellow and Director of the Technology and National Security Program, Center for a New American Security*

Dr. T. X. Hammes, *Distinguished Research Fellow, Center for Strategic Research, National Defense University*

Dr. Nicholas Murray, *Professor, U.S. Naval War College*

Christopher Zember, *Co-Director, Center for Technology and National Security Policy, National Defense University*

Appendix D. Second CSIS Roundtable Participants (October 17, 2016)

Max Angerholzer, *President and CEO, Center for the Study of the Presidency & Congress (CSPC); and Managing Director, Richard Lounsbery Foundation*

Lt. Gen. Daniel Christman (USA Ret.), *Senior Counselor to the President, U.S. Chamber of Commerce; and Former Superintendent of the United States Military Academy*

Hon. David Chu, *President and CEO, Institute for Defense Analyses; and Former Under Secretary of Defense for Personnel and Readiness*

Hon. Michael Donley, *Vice Chairman, Board of Trustees, Aerospace Corporation; and Former Secretary of the Air Force*

Hon. John Hamre, *President and CEO, Center for Strategic and International Studies; and Former Deputy Secretary of Defense*

Adam Jay Harrison, *Director, MD-5 Department of Defense Nation Security Technology Accelerator*

Gen. Paul Kern (USA Ret.), *Senior Counselor, Cohen Group; and Former Commanding General of the United States Army Materiel Command*

Lt. Gen. Ervin Rokke (USAF Ret.), *Senior Scholar, United States Air Force Academy Center for Character and Leadership Development; and Former President of the National Defense University*

Hon. Walter Slocombe, *Senior Counsel, Caplin & Drysdale; and Former Under Secretary of Defense for Policy*

Appendix E. Individuals Who Provided Input, But Did Not Participate in CSIS Roundtables

Lt. Col. Andrew Ajamian (USA), *Army Strategist (FA59) Proponent Manager, U.S. Army*

Col. Charles D. Allen (USA Ret.), *Professor of Leadership and Cultural Studies, Department of Command, Leadership, and Management, Army War College*

Hon. Brad Carson, *Acting Under Secretary of Defense for Personnel and Readiness, Office of the Secretary of Defense, Department of Defense*

Dr. Vince Connelly, *Programme Lead, Psychology, Oxford Brookes University*

Maj. Gen. Tony Cucolo (USA Ret.), *Associate Vice Chancellor for Leadership Development and Veterans Affairs, University of Texas-Austin*

Harry Foster, *Director, Center for Strategy and Technology, Air War College*

Vice Adm. Paul Gaffney (USN Ret.), *former President, Monmouth University; and former President, National Defense University*

Hon. Jacques Gansler, *Director, Center for Public Policy & Private Enterprise, University of Maryland; and former Under Secretary of Defense Acquisition, Technology & Logistics*

Adm. Edmund Giambastiani (USN Ret.), *Director, Board of Directors, The Boeing Company; and Former Vice Chairman of the Joint Chiefs of Staff*

Dr. Clark Groves (Col., USAF Ret.), *Associate Professor, National Security and Industrial Base, Eisenhower School, National Defense University*

Andrew Hunter, *Director, Defense-Industrial Initiatives Group and Senior Fellow, International Security Program, Center for International and Strategic Studies*

Dr. Bruce Jette, *President and CEO, Synovision Solutions LLC; former Director of Army Rapid Equipping Force*

Dr. Theodore R. Johnson (Cdr., USN Ret.), *Adjunct Professor, McCourt School of Public Policy, Georgetown University*

Col. Abigail Linnington (USA), *Director, Chairman's Action Group, Chairman of the Joint Chiefs of Staff*

Austin Long, *Associate Professor, School of International and Public Affairs, Columbia University*

Lt. Gen. Michael Lundy (USA), *Commanding General, U.S. Army Combined Arms Center and Fort Leavenworth, Kansas*

Adm. Michael Mullen (USN Ret.), *Charles and Marie Robertson Visiting Professor, Princeton University; and former Chairman of the Joint Chiefs of Staff*

Col. John O'Grady (USA), *Chief of Staff of the Army Senior Army Fellow, Center for Strategic and International Studies*

Dr. Michael O'Hanlon, *Senior Fellow, Brookings Institution*

Hon. Sean O'Keefe, *former Secretary of the U.S. Navy; former Administrator of the National Aeronautics and Space Administration; and University Professor, Maxwell School of Citizenship and Public Affairs, Syracuse University*

Maj. Gen. Frederick M. Padilla (USMC), *President, National Defense University*

Dr. William Roper, *Director, Strategic Capabilities Office, Office of the Secretary of Defense*

Vice Adm. Kevin Scott (USN), *Director, Joint Force Development, J7 (Pentagon)*

Adm. James Stavridis (USN Ret.), *Dean, Fletcher School of Law and Diplomacy, Tufts University*

Col. William Thigpen (USA), *Chief of Staff of the Army Senior Army Fellow, Center for Strategic and International Studies*

Lt. Gen. Richard Trefry (USA Ret.), *former Army Inspector General*

Dale C. Waters, *Director, Adaptive Execution Office, Defense Advanced Research Projects Agency*

Dr. Jerry West, *Education Advisor, Joint Staff J7, Joint Education and Doctrine Directorate Joint Professional Military Education Division*

Dr. Alexis Wichowski, *Adjunct Assistant Professor of International and Public Affairs, School of International and Public Affairs, Columbia University*

Meeting on April 18, 2016, at UK Embassy

Maj. Gen. Richard Cripwell (UK Army), *Defence Attaché*

Meetings on April 27, 2016, at Army War College

Col. Chris Beckert (USA), *Director, Center for Strategic Leadership, U.S. Army War College*

Dr. Lance Betros (Brig. Gen., USA Ret.), *Provost, U.S. Army War College*

Dr. Jeffrey Groh (Col., USA Ret.), *Professor of Information and Technology in Warfare, Department of Distance Education, U.S. Army War College*

Dr. Richard Lacquement, (Col, USA Ret.), *Dean, School of Strategic Landpower, U.S. Army War College*

Douglas C. Lovelace, Jr., *Director, Strategic Studies Institute, U.S. Army War College*

Maj. Gen. William Rapp (USA), *Commandant, U.S. Army War College*

Col. Sam White (USA Ret.), *Deputy Director, Center for Strategic Leadership, U.S. Army War College*

Meetings on May 12, 2016, at National Defense University

Dr. Michael Bell, *Chancellor, College of International Security Affairs, National Defense University*

James Churbuck, *Chair, Cyber Security Department, Information Resources Management College, National Defense University*

Rear Adm. Janice Hamby (USN Ret.), *Chancellor, Information Resources Management College, National Defense University*

Dr. Carl "Cj" Horn, *Chair, Department of Cyber Leadership and Joint Education, Information Resources Management College, National Defense University*

Dr. Feza Koprucu, *Associate Dean of Faculty, Eisenhower School*

Dr. David Tretler, *Dean of Faculty, National War College*

Dr. John D. Yaeger, *Provost, National Defense University*

Meetings on May 23, 2016, at U.S. Naval Research Laboratory

Capt. Mark Bruington (USN), *Commanding Officer, U.S. Naval Research Laboratory*

Stan Chincheck, *Director, Center for High Assurance Computer Systems, U.S. Naval Research Laboratory*

Dr. Alan Cook, *Research Physicist, U.S. Naval Research Laboratory*

Dr. Glen Henshaw, *Roboticist, U.S. Naval Research Laboratory*

Dr. Berry Jonker, *Senior Scientist, Materials Science and Technology Division, U.S. Naval Research Laboratory*

Dr. Colin Joye, *Engineer, U.S. Naval Research Laboratory*

Dr. Frank Klemm, *Superintendent, Tactical Electronic Warfare Division, U.S. Naval Research Laboratory*

Dr. John Montgomery, *Director of Research, U.S. Naval Research Laboratory*

John Pasour, *Research Physicist, U.S. Naval Research Laboratory*

Dr. Eric Snow, *Director, Institute for Nanoscience, U.S. Naval Research Laboratory*

Meetings on May 24, 2016, at U.S. Naval War College

Col. Eric Aslakson (USA), *Student, U.S. Naval War College*

Cdr. Walter Bonilla (USN Ret.), *Deputy Director, Gravely Naval Research Group, U.S. Naval War College*

Col. David Brown (USA Ret.), *Associate Professor, Advanced Naval Strategist Program (ANSP), U.S. Naval War College*

Dr. Lewis M. Duncan, *Provost, U.S. Naval War College*

Capt. James FitzSimonds (USN Ret.), *Director, Halsey Alfa Research Group, U.S. Naval War College*

Dr. Tom Gibbons, *Associate Professor of Professional Military and Graduate Education Effectiveness, U.S. Naval War College*

Dr. James E. "Jay" Hickey, *Associate Provost, U.S. Naval War College*

Vice Adm. P. Gardner Howe III (USN), *President, U.S. Naval War College*

Dr. Nicholas Murray, *Professor, Department of Strategy and Policy, U.S. Naval War College*

Michael J. Sherlock, *Professor of Academic Affairs, U.S. Naval War College*

Meetings on June 1, 2016, at Marine Corps University

Dr. James Anderson, *Vice President for Academic Affairs, Marine Corps University*

Col. Keil Gentry (USMC), *Director, Marine Corps War College*

Dr. Rebecca Johnson, *Dean, Marine Corps War College*

Dr. James Lacey, *Director, War Policy and Strategy Program, Marine Corps University*

Brig. Gen. Helen Pratt (USMC), *President, Marine Corps University*

Meeting on June 2, 2016, at CSIS, UK Director General Joint Force Development & Defence Academy

Col. Mark Cancian (USMC Ret.), *Senior Adviser, International Security Program, Center for Strategic and International Studies*

Air Vice Marshall Bruce Hedley MBE RAF (UK Royal Air Force), *Director, Joint Warfare Joint Forces Command*

Col. Stewart McConnell (UK Army), *Joint Forces Attaché*

Maj. Phil Morgan (UK Army), *Staff Officer 2, Development, UK Joint Warfare Directorate, Joint Forces Command*

Vice Adm. Duncan Potts CBE RN (UK Royal Navy), *Director General, Joint Force Development & Defence Academy*

Jeff Rathke, *Senior Fellow and Deputy Director, Europe Program, Center for Strategic and International Studies*

Meeting on June 6, 2016, at CSIS, Chief of Staff of the Army Strategic Studies Group

Col. Susan Bryant (USA), *Senior Military Fellow, Institute for National Strategic Studies, National Defense University*

Karen Burke, *RDECOM (U.S. Army Research, Development and Engineering Command), Program Analyst, Chief of Staff of the Army Strategic Studies Group*

Lt. Col. Ryan Kendall (USA), *Chief of Staff, Chief of Staff of the Army Strategic Studies Group*

Dr. Christopher Rice, *Deputy Director, Chief of Staff of the Army Strategic Studies Group*

Meetings on June 14, 2016, at Air University

Brig. Gen. Chris Coffelt (USAF), *Commandant, Air War College*

Dr. Grant Hammond, *Professor of Strategy, Center for Strategy and Technology, Air War College*

Dr. Chris Hemmer, *Dean, Air War College*

Lt. Gen. Steve Kwast (USAF), *Commander and President, Air University*

Dr. Dave Luginbuhl, *Chair, Air Force Research Laboratory; and Adjunct Faculty, Center for Strategy and Technology, Air University*

Meeting on July 26, 2016, at National Intelligence University

Dr. Brian Shaw, *Dean, Anthony G. Oettinger School of Science and Technology, National Intelligence University*

Col. Robert J. Smith, Jr. (USAF), *Associate Dean, Anthony G. Oettinger School of Science and Technology, National Intelligence University*

Dr. Susan M. Studds, *Provost, National Intelligence University*

Meeting on September 20, 2016, at CSIS, UK Director, Development, Concepts and Doctrine Centre

Scott Badenoch, *CEO, Badenoch LLC*

Col. Mark Cancian (USMC Ret.), *Senior Adviser, International Security Program, Center for Strategic and International Studies*

Col. Richard Carter (UK Army), *Assistant Head Concepts (Joint and Land), Development, Concepts and Doctrine Centre, Defence Academy of the UK*

Air Vice Marshall Bruce Hedley (UK Royal Air Force), *Director, Joint Warfare Joint Forces Command*

Col. Stewart McConnell (UK Army), *Joint Forces Attaché*

Maj. Gen. Mitch Mitchell MBE QCVS (UK Army), *Director, Development, Concepts and Doctrine Centre, Defence Academy of the UK*

Maj. Gen. Stuart Skeates (UK Army), *Commander, Standing Joint Forces HQ*

Meeting on November 14, 2016, at CSIS, UK Commander, Joint Forces Command

Capt. Paul Beattie (UK Royal Navy), *Personal Staff Officer to Commander JFC*

Gen. Sir Chris Deverell KCB MBE ADC Gen (UK Army), *Commander, Joint Forces Command*

Col. Stewart McConnell (UK Army), *Joint Forces Attaché*

Bibliography

Blog Posts/Online Commentary

McAleese, Jim. *McAleese & Associates Report*, January 26, 2016.

Books

Black, Jeremy. *War and Technology*. Bloomington, IN: Indiana University Press, 2013.

Biddle, Stephen. *Military Power: Explaining Victory and Defeat in Modern Battle*. Princeton, NJ: Princeton University Press, 2006.

Christensen, Clayton M. *The Innovator's Dilemma: The Revolutionary Book That Will Change the Way You Do Business*. New York: HarperCollins Publishers, 2003.

Halberstam, David. *The Reckoning*. New York: William Morrow and Company, 1986.

Katz, Yaakov, and Amir Bohbot. *The Weapons Wizards: How Israel Became a High-Tech Military Superpower*. New York: St. Martin's Press, 2017.

McNeill, William H. *The Pursuit of Power: Technology, Armed Force, and Society Since A.D. 1000*. Chicago, IL: University of Chicago Press, 1982.

Montfort, Nick, and Ian Bogost. *Racing the Beam: The Atari Video Computer System*. Cambridge, MA: The MIT Press, 2009.

Overy, Richard. *Why the Allies Won*. New York: W. W. Norton & Company, 1996.

Parker, Barry. *The Physics of War: From Arrows to Atoms*. Amherst, New York: Prometheus Books, 2014.

Petzold, Charles. *Code: The Hidden Language of Computer Hardware and Software*. Redmond, WA: Microsoft Press, 1999.

Sheehan, Neil. *A Fiery Peace in a Cold War: Bernard Schriever and the Ultimate Weapon*. New York: Vintage Books, 2009.

Stoll, Clifford. *The Cuckoo's Egg: Tracking a Spy through the Maze of Computer Espionage*. New York: Doubleday, 1989.

Tufte, Edward R. *The Visual Display of Quantitative Information*. Cheshire, CT: Graphics Press, 2001.

van Creveld, Martin. *Technology and War: From 2000 B.C. to the Present*. New York: The Free Press, 1991.

Zachary, G. Pascal. *Show Stopper! The Breakneck Race to Create Windows NT and the Next Generation at Microsoft*. New York: The Free Press, 1994.

Congressional Testimony

United States. Cong. Senate. Armed Services Committee. *Hearing on Increasing Effectiveness of Military Operations December 10, 2015*. 114th Cong. 1st sess. Washington, DC: GPO,

2015 (statement of Adm. James Stavridis, USN (Ret). http://www.armed-services.senate.gov/imo/media/doc/Stavridis_12-10-15.pdf.

United States. Cong. Senate. Armed Services Committee. *Hearing on the Future of Warfare November 3, 2015.* 114th Cong. 1st sess. Washington, DC: GPO, 2015 (statement of Paul Scharre). http://www.armed-services.senate.gov/imo/media/doc/Scharre_11-03-15.pdf.

United States. Cong. Senate. Armed Services Committee. *Hearing on the Future of Warfare November 3, 2015.* 114th Cong. 1st sess. Washington, DC: GPO, 2015 (statement of Dr. Peter W. Singer), http://www.armed-services.senate.gov/imo/media/doc/Singer_11-03-15.pdf.

United States. Cong. Senate. Armed Services Committee. *Hearing on Global Challenges, U.S. National Security Strategy, and Defense Organization October 22, 2015.* 114th Cong. 1st sess. Washington, DC: GPO, 2015 (statement of Professor Eliot Cohen), http://www.armed-services.senate.gov/imo/media/doc/Cohen_10-22-15.pdf.

Department of Defense Releases

"Building the First Link to the Force of the Future." Fact Sheet, November 2015.

Secretary of Defense Ashton Carter. "Force of the Future: Maintaining our Competitive Edge in Human Capital." Memorandum, November 18, 2015.

Chairman of the Joint Chiefs of Staff General Joseph Dunford Jr., USMC. "Message to the Joint Force." Memorandum, October 2, 2015, http://www.jcs.mil/portals/36/Documents/151002_CJCS_Message_to_the_Joint_Force.pdf.

Fact Sheet: Building the First Link to the Force of the Future, http://www.defense.gov/Portals/1/features/2015/0315_force-of-the-future/documents/FotF_Fact_Sheet_-_FINAL_11.18.pdf.

Fact Sheet: Recommendations for the Public Meeting on January 9, 2017, Defense Innovation Board, https://www.defense.gov/Portals/1/Documents/pubs/DIB_Recommendations_Executive_Summary_170106.pdf?ver=2017-01-10-093256-357.

Ferdinando, Lisa. "Advisory Board Approves 11 DoD Innovation Recommendations." *DoD News*, Defense Media Activity, January 9, 2017, https://www.defense.gov/News/Article/Article/1045458/advisory-board-approves-11-dod-innovation-recommendations.

Garamone, Jim. "Dunford Discusses Implications of Current Security Environment." *DoD News*, Defense Media Activity, December 14, 2015, http://www.defense.gov/News-Article-View/Article/634139/dunford-discusses-implications-of-current-security-environment.

Garamone, Jim. "Dunford to NDU Grads: Embrace Change and Innovation." *DoD News*, Defense Media Activity, June 9, 2016, http://www.defense.gov/News/Article/Article/795572/dunford-to-ndu-grads-embrace-change-and-innovation/source/GovDelivery.

Garamone, Jim. "Carter Details Force of the Future Initiatives." *DoD News*, Defense Media Activity, November 18, 2015, http://www.defense.gov/News-Article-View/Article/630400/carter-details-force-of-the-future-initiatives.

MacStravic, James A. "Final Report of the Defense Science Board Task Force on Defense Research Enterprise Assessment." Memorandum, January 27, 2017, http://www.acq.osd.mil/dsb/reports/Defense_Research_Enterprise_Assessment.pdf.

Pellerin Cheryl. "Carter: DoD Must Innovate to Lead in a Competitive World." *DoD News*, Defense Media Activity, March 1, 2016, http://www.defense.gov/News-Article-View/Article/683790/carter-dod-must-innovate-to-lead-in-a-competitive-world.

Pellerin, Cheryl. "Carter to Implement 3 Recommendations from Defense Innovation Board." *DoD News,* Defense Media Activity, October 28, 2016, https://www.defense.gov/News/Article/Article/989582/carter-to-implement-3-recommendations-from-defense-innovation-board.

Pellerin, Cheryl. "Defense Innovation Board Makes Interim Recommendations." *DoD News,* Defense Media Activity, October 5, 2016, https://www.defense.gov/News/Article/Article/965196/defense-innovation-board-makes-interim-recommendations.

Pellerin, Cheryl. "DoD Extends Technological, Operational Edge into the Future." *DoD News Features,* Defense Media Activity, December 14, 2015, http://www.defense.gov/News-Article-View/Article/634115/dod-extends-technological-operational-edge-into-the-future.

"Pentagon to Establish Defense Innovation Advisory Board." *DoD News,* Defense Media Activity, March 2, 2016, https://www.defense.gov/News/Article/Article/684366/pentagon-to-establish-defense-innovation-advisory-board.

"Secretary Carter Names Additional Members of Defense Innovation Advisory Board." Release No: NR-277-16, July 26, 2016, https://www.defense.gov/News/News-Releases/News-Release-View/Article/857710/secretary-carter-names-additional-members-of-defense-innovation-advisory-board.

"Statement by Pentagon Press Secretary Peter Cook on the Establishment of the Defense Innovation Advisory Board." Release No: NR-071-16, March 2, 2016, http://www.defense.gov/News/News-Releases/News-Release-View/Article/684201/statement-by-pentagon-press-secretary-peter-cook-on-the-establishment-of-the-de.

News Articles

Adams, John. "Don't Let China Steal the US Military's Logistical Edge." *Defense One*, March 31, 2016, http://www.defenseone.com/ideas/2016/03/dont-let-china-steal-us-militarys-logistical-edge/127155/.

Anderson, Clinton L. "Commentary: 3 Reasons to Rethink Army University." *Military Times*, November 16, 2015, http://www.militarytimes.com/story/opinion/2015/11/16/commentary-reasons-rethink-army-univ/75822152/.

Anderson, Gary. "To Beat ISIS, We Ought to Try Robotskrieg." *Small Wars Journal*, February 3, 2016, http://smallwarsjournal.com/jrnl/art/to-beat-isis-we-ought-to-try-robotskrieg.

Aslakson, Col. Eric E., and Lt. Col. (Ret.) Richard T. Brown. "Staff Colonels Are Army's Innovation Engines." Association of the United States Army, November 13, 2016, https://www.ausa.org/articles/staff-colonels-are-army%E2%80%99s-innovation-engines.

Axe, David. "The Pentagon Wants to Put This in Your Brain." *The Daily Beast*, January 23, 2016, http://www.thedailybeast.com/articles/2016/01/23/the-army-wants-to-put-this-in-your-brain.html.

Bacon, Lance M. "Marines ask science fiction enthusiasts to describe future threats." *Marine Corps Times*, February 1, 2016, http://www.marinecorpstimes.com/story/military/2016/01/30/marines-ask-science-fiction-enthusiasts-describe-future-threats/79357404/.

Bacon, Lance M. "Commandant looks to 'disruptive thinkers' to fix Corps' problems." *Marine Corps Times*, March 4, 2016, http://www.marinecorpstimes.com/story/military/2016/03/04/commandant-looks-disruptive-thinkers-fix-corps-problems/81279544/.

Barno, David, and Nora Bensahel. "Can the US Military Halt Its Brain Drain?" *The Atlantic*, November, 5, 2015, http://www.theatlantic.com/politics/archive/2015/11/us-military-tries-halt-brain-drain/413965/.

Barno, David, and Nora Bensahel. "First Steps Towards the Force of the Future." *War on the Rocks*, December 1, 2015, http://warontherocks.com/2015/12/first-steps-towards-the-force-of-the-future/.

Barno, David, and Nora Bensahel. "The Future of the Army." *Real Clear Defense*, September 22, 2016, http://www.realcleardefense.com/articles/2016/09/22/the_future_of_the_army_110105.html.

Barno, David, and Nora Bensahel. "Preparing for the Next Big War." *War on the Rocks*, January 26, 2016, http://warontherocks.com/2016/01/preparing-for-the-next-big-war/.

Betz, David. "Carnage and Connectivity: How Our Pursuit of Fun Wars Brought the Wars Home." *War on the Rocks*, February 2, 2016, http://warontherocks.com/2016/02/carnage-and-connectivity-how-our-pursuit-of-fun-wars-brought-the-wars-home/.

Bialos, Jeffrey, and Stuart Koehl. "What America's Big New Defense Plan Gets Wrong." *The National Interest*, June 1, 2016, http://nationalinterest.org/feature/what-americas-big-new-defense-plan-gets-wrong-16421.

Birkey, Doug. "Change How Air Force Buys Compass Call, JSTARS." *Breaking Defense*, May 23, 2016, http://breakingdefense.com/2016/05/change-how-air-force-buys-compass-call-jstars/#disqus_thread.

Boyd, Aaron. "Carter plugs collaboration between DoD, private sector at RSA." *Federal Times*, March 2, 2016, http://www.federaltimes.com/story/government/show-reporter/rsa2016/2016/03/02/dod-silicon-valley-collaboration/81231300/.

Brimley, Shawn, and Loren DeJonge Schulman. "Sustaining the Third Offset Strategy in the Next Administration." *War on the Rocks*, March 15, 2016, http://warontherocks.com/2016/03/sustaining-the-third-offset-strategy-in-the-next-administration/.

Brooks, Rosa. "Can There Be War without Soldiers?" *Foreign Policy*, March 15, 2016, http://foreignpolicy.com/2016/03/15/can-there-be-war-without-soldiers-weapons-cyberwarfare/.

Campobasso, Theresa. "Super Soldiers: 3D Bioprinting and the Future Fighter." *The Long War Journal*, December 8, 2015, http://smallwarsjournal.com/jrnl/art/super-soldiers-3d-bioprinting-and-the-future-fighter.

Carter, Ashton B. "Maintaining the Edge in the Age of Everything." *Defense One*, November 2, 2015, http://www.defenseone.com/ideas/2015/11/maintaining-edge-age-everything/123313/

Cavanaugh, Matt. "On Growing Strategists: Beating Back the Credentialists and the Ageists." *Modern War Institute*, April 4, 2016, http://www.modernwarinstitute.org/growing-strategists-beating-back-credentialists-ageists/#comments.

Cavanaugh, Matt. "Winter Is Coming: Sociology and the Next Great War." *Modern War Institute*, November 17, 2016, http://mwi.usma.edu/winter-coming-sociology-next-great-war/.

Cavas, Christopher P. "Dawn of the Air-Phibious Drones? Flying Fish UAV Swims and Flies." *Defense News*, February 18, 2016, http://www.defensenews.com/story/defense/show-daily/singapore-air-show/2016/02/18/air-phibious-drone-flying-fish-uav-swims-and-flies/80563292/.

Cho, Ryan. "Why the Army's Officer Evaluation System Needs a Complete Overhaul." *Task and Purpose*, December 10, 2015, http://taskandpurpose.com/why-the-armys-officer-evaluation-system-needs-a-complete-overhaul/.

Chuter, Andrew. "Britain's New Strategic Defense and Security Review Draws Praise, Caution." *Defense News*, November 25, 2015, http://www.defensenews.com/story/defense/policy-budget/budget/2015/11/25/britains-new-strategic-defense-and-security-review-draws-praise-caution/76377902/.

Chuter, Andrew. "UK To Boost Investment in Technology Innovation." *Defense News*, December 7, 2015, http://www.defensenews.com/story/defense/policy-budget/2015/12/07/uk-boost-investment-technology-innovation/76927888/.

Chuter, Andrew. "UK Eyes Nationalizing Rolls Royce Sub Engine Operations." *Defense News*, December 14, 2015, http://www.defensenews.com/story/defense/policy-budget/industry/2015/12/14/uk-eyes-nationalizing-rolls-royce-sub-engine-operations/77279856/.

Clark, Colin, and Sydney Freedberg. "Carter's Strategic Capabilities Office: Hiding in Plain Sight." *Breaking Defense*, February 5, 2016, http://breakingdefense.com/2016/02/carters-strategic-capabilities-office-arsenal-plane-missile-defense-gun/?utm_campaign=Breaking+Defense+Daily+Digest&utm_source=hs_email&utm_m

edium=email&utm_content=25955707&_hsenc=p2ANqtz-8pHDSjpBcKOs_MF0FqGm8CgOG3Nzu8VB7Vj9Tc31JjbCn0yvdJ4-PhJHUl_lr9ugWoKm8xAkY4G7QBVx5tODeyr7vwUQ&_hsmi=25955707.

Clevenger, Andrew. "Panel: DoD Needs to Evolve Its Approach to Innovation." *Defense News*, November 16, 2015, http://www.defensenews.com/story/defense/policy-budget/industry/2015/11/16/panel-dod-needs-evolve-its-approach-innovation/75880818/.

Clevenger, Andrew. "'The Terminator Conundrum': Pentagon Weighs Ethics of Pairing Deadly Force, AI." *Defense News*, January 23, 2016, http://www.defensenews.com/story/defense/policy-budget/budget/2016/01/23/terminator-conundrum-pentagon-weighs-ethics-pairing-deadly-force-ai/79205722/.

Clevenger, Andrew. "Pentagon Budget Seeks to Leverage R&D Investments." *Defense News*, February 13, 2016, http://www.defensenews.com/story/defense/policy-budget/budget/2016/02/13/pentagon-budget-seeks-leverage-rd-investments/80293508/.

Corrin, Amber. "Can DoD Regain the Technological Edge?" *C4ISR & Networks*, December 8, 2015, http://www.c4isrnet.com/story/military-tech/it/2015/12/08/can-dod-regain-the-technological-edge/76994196/.

Corrin, Amber. "5 policies that shaped the Pentagon." *Federal Times*, December 14, 2015, http://www.federaltimes.com/story/government/anniversary/2015/12/14/5-policies-shaped-pentagon/77300234/.

Corrin, Amber. "IARPA looks for new ground to cover." *C4ISR & Networks*, January 15, 2016, http://www.c4isrnet.com/story/military-tech/2016/01/15/iarpa-looks-new-ground-cover/78853110/.

Corrin, Amber. "SECDEF Carter pushes defense innovation on West Coast trip." *C4ISR & Networks*, March 2, 2016, http://www.c4isrnet.com/story/military-tech/it/2016/03/02/secdef-carter-pushes-defense-innovation-west-coast-trip/81229586/.

Corrin, Amber. "3 things on the TRADOC commander's mind." *C4ISR & Networks*, March 18, 2016, http://www.c4isrnet.com/story/military-tech/show-reporter/global-force-symposium/2016/03/17/3-things-tradoc-commanders-mind/81914158/.

Corrin, Amber. "DoD looks toward future satellites and threats." *C4ISR & Networks*, April 28, 2016, http://www.c4isrnet.com/story/military-tech/satellites/2016/04/28/dod-looks-toward-future-satellites-threats/83650110/.

Corrin, Amber. "DARPA aims to bring cutting edge to the tactical edge." *C4ISR & Networks*, May 12, 2016, http://www.c4isrnet.com/story/military-tech/it/2016/05/12/darpa-aims-bring-cutting-edge-tactical-edge/84276648/.

Davenport, Christian. "As it combats the Islamic State, Pentagon looks to assemble the force of the future." *Washington Post*, November 19, 2015,

Davenport, Christian. "Robots, swarming drones and 'Iron Man': Welcome to the new arms race." *Washington Post*, June 17, 2016, https://www.washingtonpost.com/news/checkpoint/wp/2016/06/17/robots-swarming-drones-and-iron-man-welcome-to-the-new-arms-race/.

Davis, Daniel. "Tactical at the Expense of the Strategic." *Real Clear Defense*, October 19, 2016, http://www.realcleardefense.com/articles/2016/10/19/tactical_at_the_expense_of_the_strategic_110228.html.

DeWees, Brad, and Enrique Oti. "Beyond the Power of the Coin: The Three Currencies of Military Innovation." *War on the Rocks*, July 14, 2016, http://warontherocks.com/2016/07/beyond-the-power-of-the-coin-the-three-currencies-of-military-innovation/.

DeWees, Brad. "The Military Mind in the Age of Innovation." *The Strategy Bridge*, August 9, 2016, http://thestrategybridge.org/the-bridge/2016/8/9/the-military-mind-in-the-age-of-innovation.

DeWees, Brad. "The Misconception about Innovation in the Military." *Task and Purpose*, December 14, 2015, http://taskandpurpose.com/the-misconception-about-innovation-in-the-military/.

DeWees, Brad. "A Simple 3-Step Plan For Fostering Military Innovation." *Task and Purpose*, January 5, 2016, http://taskandpurpose.com/a-simple-3-step-plan-for-fostering-military-innovation/.

DeWees, Brad. "Why Is Military Innovation so Hard?" *Task and Purpose*, February 2, 2016, http://taskandpurpose.com/why-is-military-innovation-so-hard/.

Duffy, Kevin. "Innovating the Right Way." *Small Wars Journal*, February 14, 2016, http://smallwarsjournal.com/jrnl/art/innovating-the-right-way.

Eaglen, Mackenzie. "Tech-challenged Pentagon searches for a Silicon ally." *The Wall Street Journal*, February 1, 2016, http://www.aei.org/publication/tech-challenged-pentagon-searches-for-a-silicon-ally/?utm_source=paramount&utm_medium=email&utm_content=AEITHISWEEK&utm_campaign=AEITW020616.

Eaglen, Mackenzie. "What Is the Third Offset Strategy." *Real Clear Defense*, February 16, 2016, http://www.realcleardefense.com/articles/2016/02/16/what_is_the_third_offset_strategy_109034.html.

Editorial Board. "Mr. Obama's defense budget reflects a new age of military deterrence." *Washington Post*, February 16, 2016, https://www.washingtonpost.com/opinions/mr-obamas-defense-budget-reflects-a-new-age-of-military-deterrence/2016/02/16/a0e257e0-d03c-11e5-abc9-ea152f0b9561_story.html.

Eggers, Jeff. "Forget Technology. The Real Military Edge Comes from Promoting Smart People." *Defense One*, May 4, 2016, http://www.defenseone.com/ideas/2016/05/innovation-oped/128034/?oref=d-topstory.

Erwin, Sandra I. "Defense Innovation Initiative Burdened by High Expectations." *National Defense,* November 30, 2015, http://www.nationaldefensemagazine.org/blog/Lists/Posts/Post.aspx?List=7c996cd7-cbb4-4018-baf8-8825eada7aa2&ID=2031&RootFolder=%2Fblog%2FLists%2FPosts.

Erwin, Sandra I. "Prospects for Defense Reforms in 2016 Fading Fast." *National Defense*, December 14, 2015, http://www.nationaldefensemagazine.org/blog/Lists/Posts/Post.aspx?ID=2048.

Erwin, Sandra I. "'Democratization' of Technology Rattles U.S. National Security Agencies." *National Defense*, March 2, 2016, http://www.nationaldefensemagazine.org/blog/Lists/Posts/Post.aspx?List=7c996cd7-cbb4-4018-baf8-8825eada7aa2&ID=2108&RootFolder=%2Fblog%2FLists%2FPosts.

Erwin, Sandra I. "Investing in defense technology: DoD, industry don't see eye-to-eye." *National Defense.* November 7, 2016, https://about.bgov.com/blog/investing-defense-technology-dod-industry-dont-see-eye-eye/?utm_source=newsletter&utm_medium=email&utm_content=20161110&utm_campaign=WeeklyNewsletter&bbgsum=DM-EM-BGOV-5927-NEWSLETTER.

Fallon, Michael. "Fallon: 'Britain Is Back' with 'Bigger, Stronger' Defense." *Defense News*, December 13, 2015, http://www.defensenews.com/story/defense/commentary/2015/12/13/fallon-britain-back-bigger-stronger-defense/76905922/.

Freedberg Jr., Sydney J. "DoD CIO Says Spectrum May Become Warfighting Domain." *Breaking Defense*, December 9, 2015, http://breakingdefense.com/2015/12/dod-cio-says-spectrum-may-become-warfighting-domain/.

Freedberg Jr., Sydney J. "Army Mulls Train & Advise Brigades: Gen. Milley." *Breaking Defense*, December 14, 2015, http://breakingdefense.com/2015/12/army-mulls-train-advise-brigades-gen-milley/.

Freedberg Jr., Sydney J. "Will US Pursue 'Enhanced Human Ops?' DepSecDef Wonders." *Breaking Defense*, December 14, 2015, http://breakingdefense.com/2015/12/will-us-pursue-enhanced-human-ops-depsecdef-wonders/.

Freedberg Jr., Sydney J. "Invisible Bullets: The Navy's Big Problem in Future War." *Breaking Defense*, January 27, 2016, http://breakingdefense.com/2016/01/invisible-bullets-the-navys-big-problem-in-future-war/.

Freedberg Jr., Sydney J. "Army Electronic Warfare Investment Lags Russian Threat." *Breaking Defense*, March 21, 2016, http://breakingdefense.com/2016/03/army-electronic-warfare-investment-lags-rhetoric-russians/.

Freedberg Jr., Sydney J. "McMaster: Army May Be Outnumbered AND Outgunned in Next War." *Breaking Defense*, April 6, 2016, http://breakingdefense.com/2016/04/mcmaster-army-may-be-outnumbered-and-outgunned-in-next-war/.

Frost, Patricia, and Matthew Hutchison. "Top 10 Questions for Commanders to Ask about Cybersecurity." *Small Wars Journal,* December 8, 2015, http://smallwarsjournal.com/jrnl/art/top-10-questions-for-commanders-to-ask-about-cybersecurity?utm_source=twitterfeed&utm_medium=twitter.

Gady, Franz-Stefan. "Pentagon Wants 'Arsenal Planes' to Beat China's Air Defenses." *The Diplomat*, February 16, 2016, http://thediplomat.com/2016/02/pentagon-wants-arsenal-planes-to-beat-chinas-air-defenses/.

Gady, Franz-Stefan. "Why We Need Philosophers in the Pentagon." *The Diplomat,* November 16, 2016, http://thediplomat.com/2016/11/why-we-need-philosophers-in-the-pentagon/?utm_source=RealClearDefense+Morning+Recon&utm_campaign=4266c1cd9c-EMAIL_CAMPAIGN_2016_11_18&utm_medium=email&utm_term=0_694f73a8dc-4266c1cd9c-83953533.

Gilli, Andrea, and Mauro Gilli. "So what if Iranian drones did strike Syria? We are not entering a dark age of robotic warfare." *Washington Post*, April 4, 2016, https://www.washingtonpost.com/news/monkey-cage/wp/2016/04/04/so-what-if-iranian-drones-did-strike-syria-we-are-not-entering-a-dark-age-of-robotic-warfare/.

Ginsberg, Daniel, and Ray Conley. "Commentary: Investing in military human capital." *Army Times*, November 3, 2015, http://www.armytimes.com/story/opinion/2015/11/03/commentary-investing-military-human-capital/75083840/http://www.armytimes.com/story/opinion/2015/11/03/commentary-investing-military-human-capital/75083840/.

Gould, Joe. "Experts: Pentagon's Tech Edge Faltering." *Defense News*, December 1, 2015, http://www.defensenews.com/story/defense/policy-budget/warfare/2015/12/01/experts-pentagons-tech-edge-faltering/76620638/.

Gould, Joe, and Aaron Mehta. "Pentagon, Top Lawmakers Craft DoD Reforms." *Defense News*, March 6, 2016, http://www.defensenews.com/story/defense/policy-budget/2016/03/04/pentagon-top-lawmakers-craft-dod-reforms/81310216/.

Gould, Joe. "Thornberry: Acquisition Reform Bill Aims at Innovation." *Defense News*, March 16, 2016, http://www.defensenews.com/story/defense/2016/03/16/thornberry-acquisition-reform-bill-aims-innovation/81846940/.

Gouré, Daniel. "The End of America's Competitive Military Advantage." Lexington Institute, October 29, 2015, http://lexingtoninstitute.org/the-end-of-americas-competitive-military-advantage/.

Gouré, Daniel. "The Future of Conflict and the U.S. Army's Big 8 Initiative." *Real Clear Defense*, March 18, 2016, http://www.realcleardefense.com/articles/2016/03/18/the_future_of_conflict_and_the_us_armys_big_8_initiative_109156.html.

Gourley, Scott. "Stimulating Simulation: Technology Advances and Upgrades Boost Realism in Soldier Training." *Army Magazine*, February 16, 2016, http://www.armymagazine.org/2016/02/16/stimulating-simulation-technology-advances-and-upgrades-boost-realism-in-soldier-training/.

Grady, John. "Senate Panel Explores Speed of U.S. Military Technology, Weapons Development." *USNI News*, November 3, 2015, http://news.usni.org/2015/11/03/senate-panel-explores-speed-of-u-s-military-technology-weapons-development.

Grady, John. "Panel Suggests Pentagon Quadrennial Defense Review Changes to Senate." *USNI News*, December 8, 2015, http://news.usni.org/2015/12/08/panel-suggests-pentagon-quadrennial-defense-review-changes-to-senate.

Hale, Robert, and Ronald Sanders. "Developing Civilian Leaders in DoD." *Defense News*, January 26, 2016, http://www.defensenews.com/story/defense/commentary/2016/01/26/developing-civilian-leaders-dod/79055042/.

Hammes, T.X. "In an Era of Cheap Drones, US Can't Afford Exquisite Weapons." *Defense One*, January 19, 2016, http://www.defenseone.com/ideas/2016/01/cheap-drones-exquisite-weapons/125216/.

Hammes, T.X. "Commentary: Technology Converges, Power Diffuses." *Defense News*, February 15, 2016, http://www.defensenews.com/story/defense/commentary/2016/02/15/commentary-technology-converges-power-diffuses/79772380/.

Hardy, Michael. "Moon landing: U.S. cements its S&T domination." *Federal Times*, November 30, 2015, http://www.federaltimes.com/story/government/anniversary/2015/11/30/moon-landing-us-cements-its-st-domination/76365222/.

Hardy, Michael. "From sci-fi to real life: Government's changing role in tech innovation." *C4ISR & Networks*, January 4, 2016, http://www.c4isrnet.com/story/military-tech/it/2016/01/04/sci-fi-real-life-governments-changing-role-tech-innovation/78263802/.

Hardy, Michael. "Pentagon proves air-launched UAV swarm ability." *C4ISR & Networks*, March 15, 2016, http://www.c4isrnet.com/story/military-tech/uas/2016/03/15/pentagon-proves-uav-swarm-ability/81803256/.

Hardy, Quentin. "Silicon Valley Looks to Artificial Intelligence for the Next Big Thing." *New York Times*, March 28, 2016.

Harper, John. "2017 Budget Proposal to Include Billions for Next-Generation Weapons Research." *National Defense*, December 14, 2015, http://www.nationaldefensemagazine.org/blog/Lists/Posts/Post.aspx?List=7c996cd7-cbb4-4018-baf8-8825eada7aa2&ID=2049&RootFolder=%2Fblog%2FLists%2FPosts.

Harper, John. "Defense Department Moving Slowly on 'Internet of Things.'" *National Defense*, January 19, 2016, http://www.nationaldefensemagazine.org/archive/2016/February/Pages/DefenseDepartmentMovingSlowlyonInternetofThings.aspx.

Hempel, Jessi. "Department of Defense Head Ashton Carter Enlists Silicon Valley to Transform the Military." *Wired*, November 18, 2015, http://www.wired.com/2015/11/secretary-of-defense-ashton-carter/.

Hoffman, Frank. "Friendly Fire: The Risks and Rewards of Red Teaming." *War on the Rocks*, November 4, 2015, http://warontherocks.com/2015/11/friendly-fire-the-risks-and-rewards-of-red-teaming/.

Hoffman, Michael. "Commentary: Silicon Valley Innovators Want to Tackle Pentagon Problems." *Defense News*, December 15, 2015, http://www.defensenews.com/story/defense/commentary/2015/12/15/commentary-silicon-valley-innovators-want-tackle-pentagon-problems/77351844/.

Hoffman, Michael. "Army Sees Lasers, Hoverbikes and Nano Drones in Future Force." Military.com, March 17, 2016, http://www.military.com/daily-news/2016/03/17/army-sees-lasers-hoverbikes-and-nano-drones-in-future-force.html.

Jamali, Naveed. "Why the military needs unorthodox career tracks — now." *Navy Times*, May 1, 2016, http://www.navytimes.com/story/opinion/2016/04/29/why-military-needs-unorthodox-career-tracks-now/83199886/.

Johnson, Theodore R. "Will the Department of Defense Invest in People or Technology?" *The Atlantic,* November 29, 2015, http://www.theatlantic.com/politics/archive/2016/11/trump-military-third-offset-strategy/508964/.

Jones, Joshua. "Play On: Supporting Decision-Makers by Sustaining Wargaming." *War on the Rocks,* April 15, 2016, http://warontherocks.com/2016/04/play-on-supporting-decision-makers-by-sustaining-wargaming/.

Judson, Jen. "As Army Shrinks, Milley Considers Ways to Regenerate Force." *Defense News*, December 15, 2015, http://www.defensenews.com/story/defense/land/2015/12/14/army-shrinks-milley-considers-ways-regenerate-force/77308854/.

Judson, Jen. "US Army Putting Finishing Touches on Autonomous Systems Strategy." *Defense News*, March 17, 2016, http://www.defensenews.com/story/defense/show-daily/ausa-global-force/2016/03/17/army-autonomous-system-strategy/81897736/.

Kar, Ian. "NATO and the Pentagon Want to Get Their Hands on the Technology Behind Bitcoin." *Defense One*, May 11, 2016, http://www.defenseone.com/technology/2016/05/nato-and-pentagon-want-get-their-hands-technology-behind-bitcoin/128203/.

Lacey, James. "Wargaming in the Classroom: An Odyssey." *War on the Rocks*, April 28, 2016, http://warontherocks.com/2016/04/wargaming-in-the-classroom-an-odyssey/.

Lacovelli, Niccolo. "A Greater Challenge Is Needed for Cyber Forces." Modern War Institute, February 28, 2016, http://www.modernwarinstitute.org/a-greater-challenge-needed-for-cyber-forces/#comments.

LaGrone, Sam. "Little Known Pentagon Office Key to U.S. Military Competition with China, Russia." *U.S. Naval Institute News*, February 2, 2016, http://news.usni.org/2016/02/02/little-known-pentagon-office-key-to-u-s-military-competition-with-china-russia.

Lamothe, Dan. "Veil of secrecy lifted on Pentagon office planning 'Avatar' fighters and drone swarms." *Washington Post*, March 8, 2016, https://www.washingtonpost.com/news/checkpoint/wp/2016/03/08/inside-the-secretive-pentagon-office-planning-skyborg-fighters-and-drone-swarms/.

Lin, Jeffrey, and P.W. Singer. "China to Launch World's Most Powerful Hyperspectral Satellite." *Popular Science*, January 25, 2016, http://www.popsci.com/china-to-launch-worlds-most-powerful-hyperspectral-satellite.

Lopez, Ciro. "Four Steps Leaders Can Take to Create an Innovative Climate." U.S. Naval Institute Blog, March 2016, https://blog.usni.org/2016/03/28/four-steps-leaders-can-take-to-create-an-innovative-climate.

Majumdar, Dave. "Revealed: Pentagon's Plan to Defeat Russian and Chinese Radar with A.I." *The National Interest*, February 29, 2016, http://nationalinterest.org/blog/the-buzz/revealed-pentagons-plan-defeat-russian-chinese-radar-ai-15357.

Markoff, John. "Pentagon Shops in Silicon Valley for Game Changers." *New York Times*, February 26, 2015, http://www.nytimes.com/2015/02/27/science/pentagon-looking-for-edge-in-the-future-checks-in-with-silicon-valley.html?emc=edit_tnt_20150226&nlid=50190688&tntemail0=y&_r=0.

Markoff, John. "Report Cites Dangers of Autonomous Weapons." *New York Times*, February 28, 2016, http://mobile.nytimes.com/2016/02/29/technology/report-cites-dangers-of-autonomous-weapons.html?emc=edit_tnt_20160228&nlid=50190688&tntemail0=y&_r=1&referer=.

Markoff, John, and Matthew Rosenberg. "The Pentagon's 'Terminator Conundrum': Robots That Could Kill on Their Own." *New York Times,* October 25, 2016, http://www.nytimes.com/2016/10/26/us/pentagon-artificial-intelligence-terminator.html.

Massie, Andy. "Reframing the Third Offset as a 21st-century Model for Deterrence." *War on the Rocks*, March 28, 2016, http://warontherocks.com/2016/03/reframing-the-third-offset-as-a-21st-century-model-for-deterrence/.

Mauer, Dan. "The 'Inception' Theory of Military Innovation." Modern Institute of War, March 29, 2016, http://www.modernwarinstitute.org/inception-theory-military-innovation/.

McLaughlin, John. "US Strategy and Strategic Culture from 2017." *Global Brief*, February 19, 2016, http://globalbrief.ca/blog/2016/02/19/american-strategy-and-strategic-culture-%E2%80%93-next-administration/.

Mehta, Aaron. "Carter Unveils Budget Details; Pentagon Requests $582.7 Billion." *Military Times*, February 2, 2016, http://www.militarytimes.com/story/breaking-news/2016/02/02/carter-unveils-budget-details-pentagon-requests-5827b-funding/79686138/.

Mehta, Aaron. "Space, Munitions Among Next Wave of Pentagon Strategic Portfolio Reviews." *Defense News*, February 8, 2016, http://www.defensenews.com/story/defense/policy-budget/2016/02/08/space-munitions-offset-russia-china-strategic-portfolio-reviews/80008806/.

Mehta, Aaron. "Carter Heads to Silicon Valley as ISIS Cyberwar Expands." *Defense News*, February 29, 2016, http://www.defensenews.com/story/defense/innovation/2016/02/29/ash-carter-silicon-valley-isis-cyberwar-san-francisco-rsa/81110598/.

Mehta, Aaron. "At Silicon Valley Outpost, Carter Hears Pitches from Small Firms." *Defense News*, March 3, 2016, http://www.defensenews.com/story/defense/innovation/2016/03/03/diux-shark-tank-silicon-valley-as-carter-small-firms/81244834/.

Mehta, Aaron. "Carter Gets Strong Marks for Innovation Push; Challenges Remain." *Defense News*, March 5, 2016, http://www.defensenews.com/story/defense/innovation/2016/03/05/ash-carter-eric-schmidt-innovation-push-san-francisco-rsa/81272708/.

Mehta, Aaron. "Strategic Capabilities Office Looks for Industry Feedback." *Defense News*, March 28, 2016, http://www.defensenews.com/story/defense/innovation/2016/03/28/strategic-capabilities-office-sco-industry-feedback-arsenal-plane-sm6-pentagon/82356496/.

Mehta, Aaron. "DIUX Expands to Boston, with New Leadership." *Defense News*, May 11, 2016, http://www.defensenews.com/story/defense-news/techwatch/2016/05/11/diux-expands-boston-new-leadership/84233338/.

Michel, Leo. "British Defense: Mind the Gap." *NATOSource*, December 8, 2015, http://www.atlanticcouncil.org/blogs/natosource/british-defense-mind-the-gap.

Miller, David T. "The National Intelligence Council: The Upcoming Global Trends 2035 Report." *Small Wars Journal*, May 30, 2016, http://smallwarsjournal.com/jrnl/art/the-national-intelligence-council-the-upcoming-global-trends-2035-report.

Mulrine, Anna. "Why America isn't winning its wars." *Christian Science Monitor*, December 12, 2015, http://www.csmonitor.com/USA/Military/2015/1211/Why-America-isn-t-winning-its-wars.

Murphy, Mike. "The US Military is Developing Brain Implants to Boost Memory and Heal PTSD." *Defense One*, November 17, 2015, http://www.defenseone.com/technology/2015/11/us-military-developing-brain-implants-boost-memory-and-heal-ptsd/123784/.

Murphy, Mike. "America's Spies Want to Speed Up IBM's Quest for a Quantum Computer." *DefenseOne*, December 9, 2015, http://www.defenseone.com/technology/2015/12/americas-spies-want-speed-ibms-quest-quantum-computer/124334/?oref=d_brief_nl.

Murray, Nicholas. "Rigor in Joint Professional Military Education." *War on the Rocks*, February 17, 2016, http://warontherocks.com/2016/02/rigor-in-joint-professional-military-education/.

Olson, Eric. "America's Not Ready for Today's Gray Wars." *Defense One*, December 10, 2015, http://www.defenseone.com/ideas/2015/12/americas-not-ready-todays-gray-wars/124381/.

Peck, Michael. "Gray Eagle performs manned-unmanned teaming in South Korea." *C4ISR & Networks*, December 1, 2015, http://www.c4isrnet.com/story/military-tech/uas/2015/12/01/gray-eagle-performs-manned-unmanned-teaming-south-korea/76604074/.

Peck, Michael. "DARPA awards Squad X contract." *C4ISR & Networks*, December 14, 2015, http://www.c4isrnet.com/story/military-tech/sensors/2015/12/14/darpa-awards-squad-x-contract/77303926/.

Peck, Michael. "DARPA wants to link brains to digital world." *C4ISR & Networks*, February 1, 2016, http://www.c4isrnet.com/story/military-tech/it/2016/02/01/darpa-wants-link-brains-digital-world/79655474/.

Peck, Michael. "DARPA expands Squad X program." *C4ISR & Networks*, March 22, 2016, http://www.c4isrnet.com/story/military-tech/sensors/2016/03/22/darpa-squad-x-experimentation-program/82111594/.

Perkins, Jim. "Inspire, Connect, and Empower: A Network of Defense Intrapreneurs." *War on the Rocks,* July 15, 2016, http://warontherocks.com/2016/07/inspire-connect-and-empower-a-network-of-defense-intrapreneurs/.

Philpott, Tom. "Military Update: Carter's 'Force of the Future' Tallies Only Modest Changes." *Stars and Stripes*, November 19, 2015, http://www.stripes.com/military-update-carter-s-force-of-the-future-tallies-only-modest-changes-1.379653.

Philpott, Tom. "Military Update: Force of the Future might survive attack on its architect." *Colorado Springs Gazette*, March 6, 2016, http://gazette.com/military-update-force-of-the-future-might-survive-attack-on-its-architect/article/1571575.

Pietrucha, Mike. "The U.S. Air Force and Stealth: Stuck on Denial Pt. 1." *War on the Rocks*, March 24, 2016, http://warontherocks.com/2016/03/stuck-on-denial-part-i-the-u-s-air-force-and-stealth/.

Preston, Bradley. "Work: The Age of Everything Is the Era of Grand Strategy." *Defense One*, November 2, 2015, http://www.defenseone.com/management/2015/11/work-age-everything-era-grand-strategy/123335/.

Quintas, Lee. "The Future Is Now. Is the Army Ready?" *War on the Rocks*, December 10, 2015, http://warontherocks.com/2015/12/the-future-is-now-is-the-army-ready/.

Ravindranath, Mohana. "Watchdog: Too Many DARPA Projects Enter 'Valley of Death,' Don't Progress." *Nextgov*, November 25, 2015, http://www.nextgov.com/emerging-tech/2015/11/watchdog-darpa-needs-improve-tech-transition-tracking/124011/.

Scharre, Paul. "Precision-Guided Weapons Come to the Infantry." *War on the Rocks*, November 11, 2015, http://warontherocks.com/2015/11/precision-guided-weapons-come-to-the-infantry/.

Scott, Richard. "UK invites bids for laser weapon demonstrator." *IHS Jane's 360*, December 14, 2015, http://www.janes.com/article/56622/uk-invites-bids-for-laser-weapon-demonstrator.

Richardson, Erik. "Beyond Ender: Amplified Intelligence and the Age of the School Wars." *Small Wars Journal,* October 23, 2016, http://smallwarsjournal.com/jrnl/art/beyond-ender-amplified-intelligence-and-the-age-of-the-school-wars.

Seck, Hope Hodge. "Corps' Warfighting Strategy Update to Focus on High-Tech Fights." Military.com, March 16, 2016, http://www.military.com/daily-news/2016/03/16/corps-warfighting-strategy-update-to-focus-on-high-tech-fights.html.

Seligman, Lara. "Analysts, Lawmakers Urge DoD to Rethink Electronic Warfare." *Defense* News, December 2, 2015, http://www.defensenews.com/story/defense/air-space/isr/2015/12/02/analysts-lawmakers-urge-dod-rethink-electronic-warfare/76670716/.

Seligman, Lara. "The Air Force of the Future: Lasers on Fighter Jets, Planes That Think." *Defense News*, February 20, 2016, http://www.defensenews.com/story/defense/air-space/2016/02/20/air-force-future-lasers-fighter-jets-planes-think/80515698/.

Shane III, Leo. "Military promotions need an overhaul next, experts say." *Military Times*, December 2, 2015, http://www.militarytimes.com/story/military/capitol-hill/2015/12/02/military-promotions-overhaul-ideas/76663106/.

SIG Scouting Report for the week of November 23, 2015. "Human-Machine Collaboration: Planning for the Future."

Sisk, Richard. "DoD to Expand 'Force of the Future' Personnel Plan Despite Setback." Military.com, March 15, 2016, http://www.military.com/daily-news/2016/03/15/dod--expand-force-of-the-future-personnel-plan-despite-setback.html.

Steinman, Joshua. "Imagine the Starling: Peak Fighter, the Swarm, and the Future of Air Combat." *War on the Rocks*, February 17, 2016, http://warontherocks.com/2016/02/imagine-the-starling-peak-fighter-the-swarm-and-the-future-of-air-combat/.

Swarts, Phillip. "Hypersonic missiles could be operational in 2020s, general says." *Air Force Times*, February 26, 2016, http://www.airforcetimes.com/story/military/2016/02/26/hypersonic-missiles-could-operational-2020s-general-says/80993654/.

Swarts, Phillip. "Hypersonics could help Air Force thwart enemy anti-air defenses." *Air Force Times*, March 1, 2016, http://www.airforcetimes.com/story/military/2016/03/01/hypersonics-could-help-us-air-force-thwart-enemy-anti-air-defenses/81156854/.

Tama, Jordan. "Why Strategic Planning Matters to National Security." *Lawfare*, March 6, 2016, https://www.lawfareblog.com/why-strategic-planning-matters-national-security.

Tan, Michelle. "Top Army general outlines plans for new brigades, new technologies." *Army Times*, January 21, 2016, http://www.armytimes.com/story/military/pentagon/2016/01/21/army-chief-outlines-plans-new-brigades-new-technologies/79129834/.

Tan, Michelle. "US Army Seeks Faster Innovation, Capabilities for the Future." *Defense News*, March 17, 2016, http://www.defensenews.com/story/defense/show-daily/ausa-global-force/2016/03/17/us-army-seeks-faster-innovation-capabilities-future/81912744/.

Taylor, Adam, and Laris Karklis. "This remarkable chart shows how U.S. defense spending dwarfs the rest of the world." *Washington Post*, February 9, 2016, https://www.washingtonpost.com/news/worldviews/wp/2016/02/09/this-remarkable-chart-shows-how-u-s-defense-spending-dwarfs-the-rest-of-the-world/.

Tilghman, Andrew. "SecDef pulls back on personnel reforms, leaves out big changes for now." *Military Times*, November 19, 2015, http://www.militarytimes.com/story/military/benefits/2015/11/18/secdef-pulls-back-personnel-reforms-leaves-out-big-changes/76004136/.

Tilghman, Andrew. "Joint Billet Requirements, Chain of Command Under Review." *Military Times*, December 9, 2015, http://www.militarytimes.com/story/military/pentagon/2015/12/08/carter-review-goldwater-nichols/76998526/.

Tilghman, Andrew. "At West Point, millennial cadets say rigid military career tracks are outdated." *Military Times*, March 27, 2016, http://www.militarytimes.com/story/military/careers/2016/03/26/west-point-millenials-military-careers/82261372/.

Thompson, Loren. "Gene Wars: Targeted Mutations Will Spawn Unique Dangers, and Soon." *Forbes*, January 29, 2016, http://www.forbes.com/sites/lorenthompson/2016/01/29/gene-wars-targeted-mutations-will-spawn-unique-dangers-and-soon/#20293a4d41d0.

Thornhill, Paula. "Do 'Guardian Forces' Belong in the Military?" *Defense One*, March 9, 2016, http://www.defenseone.com/ideas/2016/03/guardian-forces-military-cyber-space/126564/?oref=d_brief_nl.

Tucker, Patrick. "These Are the New Weapons the Pentagon Chief Wants for Tomorrow's Wars." *Defense One*, February 2, 2016, http://www.defenseone.com/technology/2016/02/New-weapons-pentagon-wants-tomorrows-wars/125611/.

Tucker, Patrick. "New Microchip Could Increase Military Intelligence Powers Exponentially." *Defense One*, February 4, 2016, http://www.defenseone.com/technology/2016/02/new-microchip-could-increase-military-intelligence-powers-exponentially/125715/?oref=d_brief_nl.

Tucker, Patrick. "The Army Has Made a Robot Cockroach." *Defense One*, February 8, 2016, http://www.defenseone.com/technology/2016/02/army-has-made-robot-cockroach/125766/?oref=defenseone_today_nl.

Tucker, Patrick. "We're on the Same Side, Carter Tells Silicon Valley." *Defense One*, March 1, 2016, http://www.defenseone.com/technology/2016/03/were-same-side-carter-tells-silicon-valley/126335/.

Tucker, Patrick. "America's New Special Operations Commander Wants to Predict the Future." *Defense One*, May 25, 2016, http://www.defenseone.com/threats/2016/05/americas-new-special-operations-commander-wants-predict-future/128583/?oref=defenseone_today_nl.

Tucker, Patrick. "The Problem with the Pentagon's Hypersonic Missile." *Defense One*, April 14, 2016, http://www.defenseone.com/technology/2016/04/problem-pentagon-hypersonic-missile/127493/?oref=d-mostread.

Ullman, Harlan, and James Stavridis. "Needed: A Revolution in US Military Education." *Defense News*, December 14, 2015.

"US Army to develop laser weapons by 2023." *Army-Technology*, February 29, 2016, http://www.army-technology.com/news/newsus-army-to-develop-laser-weapons-by-2023-4824448.

Watson, Ben. "Hey, America: Don't Forget Your Soldiers While Spending Billions on Future Weapons." *Defense One*, March 14, 2016, http://www.defenseone.com/ideas/2016/03/america-dont-forget-your-soldiers-spending-billions-future-weapons/126646/.

Weisgerber, Marcus. "Pentagon Wants to Pair Troops with Machines to Deter Russia, China." *Defense One*, November 8, 2015, http://www.defenseone.com/technology/2015/11/pentagon-wants-pair-troops-machines-deter-russia-china/123498/.

Whittle, Richard. "Finmeccanica Unit Claims Counter-Drone Breakthrough." *Breaking Defense*, January 19, 2016, http://breakingdefense.com/2016/01/finmeccanica-unit-claims-counter-drone-breakthrough/.

Deputy Secretary of Defense Work, Bob, and Gen. Paul Selva. "Revitalizing Wargaming Is Necessary to Be Prepared for Future Wars." *War on the Rocks*, December 8, 2015, http://warontherocks.com/2015/12/revitalizing-wargaming-is-necessary-to-be-prepared-for-future-wars/.

Journal Articles

Aslakson, Col. Eric E. "The Army Is Falling Short in Developing Creative Leaders." *Army Magazine*, May 2016, 66:5, pp. 19-20, http://www.armymagazine.org/2016/04/27/the-army-is-falling-short-in-developing-creative-leaders/.

Gilli, Andrea, and Mauro Gilli. "The Diffusion of Drone Warfare? Industrial, Organizational, and Infrastructural Constraints." *Security Studies,* April 2016, 25:1, pp. 50–84.

Hammes, T.X. "Technology Converges, Power Diffuses: The Evolution of Small, Smart, and Cheap Weapons." Cato Institute Policy Analysis no. 786, January 27, 2016, https://www.cato.org/publications/policy-analysis/technologies-converge-power-diffuses-evolution-small-smart-cheap.

Jenzen-Jones, N.R. "Chambering the Next Round: Emergent Small-calibre Cartridge Technologies." *Small Arms Survey*, February 2016, http://www.smallarmssurvey.org/fileadmin/docs/F-Working-papers/SAS-WP23-cartridge-technologies.pdf.

Liou, Yu-Ming, Paul Musgrave, and J. Furman Daniel III. "The Imitation Game: Why Don't Rising Powers Innovate Their Militaries More?" *Washington Quarterly*, Fall 2015, 38:3 pp. 157–74.

McMaster, Lt. Gen. H. R. "Continuity and Change the Army Operating Concept and Clear Thinking about Future War." *Military Review*, March–April 2015, pp. 6–21, http://usacac.army.mil/CAC2/MilitaryReview/Archives/English/MilitaryReview_20150430_art001.pdf.

Ullman, Harlan. "An Effective Brains Based Strategy for the 21st Century." July 16, 2015.

Waddell, Capt. Joshua. "Innovation: And Other Things That Brief Well." *Marine Corps Gazette*, February 2017, 101:2, https://www.mca-marines.org/gazette/2017/02/innovation?utm_source=RealClearDefense+Morning+Recon&utm_campaign=e37911a460-EMAIL_CAMPAIGN_2017_02_08&utm_medium=email&utm_term=0_694f73a8dc-e37911a460-83953533.

Warren, Jason. "The Centurion Mindset and the Army's Strategic Leader Paradigm." *Parameters*, Autumn 2015, 45:3, pp. 27–38, http://www.strategicstudiesinstitute.army.mil/pubs/parameters/issues/Autumn_2015/6_Warren.pdf.

Weinberger, Sharon. 2014. "The Evolving Science of War." *Nature* 505 (7482): 156–57.

Reports

Brimley, Shawn. "While We Can: Arresting the Erosion of America's Military Edge." Center for a New American Security, December 2015, http://www.cnas.org/sites/default/files/publications-pdf/While%20We%20Can-151207.pdf.

Cancian, Mark F., and Todd Harrison. "The Force of the Future." Center for Strategic and International Studies, November 19, 2015, http://csis.org/publication/force-future.

Committee on Homeland and National Security of the National Science and Technology Council. "A 21st Century Science, Technology, and Innovation Strategy for America's National Security." Executive Office of the President, May 2016, https://www.whitehouse.gov//sites/default/files/microsites/ostp/NSTC/national_security_s_and_t_strategy.pdf.

Defense Business Board. "Innovation: Attracting and Retaining the Best of the Private Sector." 2014, http://dbb.defense.gov/Portals/35/Documents/Reports/2014/DBB-FY14-02-Innovation%20report%20(final).pdf.

FitzGerald, Ben, Alexandra Sander, and Jacqueline Parziale. "Future Foundry: A New Strategic Approach to Military-Technical Advantage." Center for a New American Security, December 2016, https://www.cnas.org/publications/reports/future-foundry.

Fitzgerald, Ben, and Loren DeJonge Schulman. "12 MONTHS IN – 8 MONTHS LEFT: An Update on Secretary Carter's Innovation Agenda." Center for a New American Security, April 2016, http://www.cnas.org/sites/default/files/publications-pdf/CNASReport-InnovationMemo-160428.pdf.

Hamre, John. "Reflections: Looking Back at the Need for Goldwater-Nichols." Center for Strategic and International Studies, January 27, 2016, http://defense360.csis.org/goldwater-nichols-2016/.

Hunter, Andrew. "Making Innovation Great." Center for Strategic and International Studies, January 2017, https://defense360.csis.org/making-innovation-great/.

Kamarck, Kristy N. "Goldwater-Nichols and the Evolution of Officer Joint Professional Military Education (JPME)." *Congressional Research Service Report,* January 13, 2016, https://www.fas.org/sgp/crs/natsec/R44340.pdf.

Miller, David T. *Defense 2045: Assessing the Future Security Environment and Implications for Defense Policymakers."* Center for Strategic and International Studies, November 2015, https://www.csis.org/analysis/defense-2045.

Olson, Major Stephen E. USAF. "Iron Sharpens Iron: A Comparative Study of the Advanced Military Studies Program and the School of Advanced Air and Space Studies." School of Advanced Military Studies, United States Army Command and General Staff College, Academic Year 2012.

Sayler, Kelly. "RED ALERT: The Growing Threat to U.S. Aircraft Carriers." Center for a New American Security, February 2016, http://www.cnas.org/sites/default/files/publications-pdf/CNASReport-CarrierThreat-160217.pdf.

Scharre, Paul. "Uncertain Ground: Emerging Challenges in Land Warfare." Center for a New American Security, December 2015, http://www.cnas.org/sites/default/files/publications-pdf/CNAS%20Report_Uncertain%20Ground_151203%20v02.pdf.

Scharre, Paul. "Autonomous Weapons and Operational Risk." Center for a New American Security, February 2016, http://www.cnas.org/sites/default/files/publications-pdf/CNAS_Autonomous-weapons-operational-risk.pdf.

Stillion, John. "Trends in Air-to-Air Combat: Implications for Future Air Superiority." Center for Strategic and Budgetary Assessments, April 2015, http://csbaonline.org/publications/2015/04/trends-in-air-to-air-combat-implications-for-future-air-superiority/.

Zheng, Denise E., and William A. Carter. *Leveraging the Internet of Things for a More Efficient and Effective Military*. Center for Strategic and International Studies, September 2015.

About the Authors

Raymond F. DuBois is a senior adviser at CSIS, where he focuses on international security policy, civil-military relations, joint professional military education, and defense management reform. He served as acting under secretary of the army from February 2005 to February 2006. From October 2002 to May 2005, he was director of administration and management, and concurrently, director of Washington Headquarters Services. From April 2001 through November 2004, DuBois served as the deputy under secretary of defense for installations and environment. His prior service in the Pentagon was from 1973 to 1977, when he was a staff assistant to the secretary of defense, followed by service on a special task force for Southeast Asia as special assistant to the Pentagon comptroller, followed by assignment as special assistant to the secretary of the army and as deputy under secretary of the army. He served in the U.S. Army from 1967 to 1969, including nearly 13 months in Vietnam as a combat intelligence operations sergeant in the Central Highlands, where he received the Army Commendation Medal. Mr. DuBois currently serves as a global senior adviser to McKinsey & Co. and on the International Advisory Council of the U.S. Institute of Peace, and he lectures at the Marine Corps War College. Mr. DuBois received a B.A. degree from Princeton University in 1972.

Daniel M. Gerstein works at the RAND Corporation and is an adjunct professor at American University. Previously, he served at the U.S. Department of Homeland Security (DHS) as under secretary (acting) and deputy under secretary in the Science & Technology Directorate. Gerstein began his professional career in the U.S. Army, serving on four continents, participating in combat, peacekeeping, humanitarian assistance, counterterrorism, and homeland security. Following retirement from active duty, he joined L-3 Corporation as vice president for homeland security services. Before joining DHS, Gerstein was the principal director for countering WMD in OSD (Policy). He has authored books and articles on national security topics and is a member of the Council on Foreign Relations. He graduated from West Point and has masters' degrees from Georgia Tech, National Defense University, and Army Command & General Staff College, and a Ph.D. from George Mason University.

James M. Keagle is university professor at the Eisenhower School of the National Defense University (NDU). He formerly served as director and deputy director of the Emerging Challenges Program at the Center for Technology and National Security Policy at NDU. Dr. Keagle also served for nine years as NDU's provost and vice president for academic affairs, as well as professor of national security strategy. He is a graduate of the U.S. Air Force Academy and holds an M.A. in political science with a certificate in Latin American studies from the University of Pittsburgh and both an M.A. and Ph.D. in politics from Princeton University. He received an honorary doctorate from the Military Technical Academy of Romania.

Rose Morrissy is a research assistant to Raymond DuBois at CSIS. She holds an M.A. from the Maxwell School of Citizenship and Public Affairs at Syracuse University and a B.A. from the University of Illinois at Urbana-Champaign.